CAPPY'S JOURNAL

Gary Leon Zimmer

Copyright © 2018 Gary Leon Zimmer All rights reserved. No part of this book may be reproduced in any form or by any electronic or mechanical means—except in the case of brief quotations embodied in articles or reviews—without written permission from the publisher. Copyright © 2018 Gary Leon Zimmer All rights reserved.

ISBN—9781644679876

Acknowledgements:

Cappy's Journal is the celebration of a life well-lived! The first acknowledgement and the first credit is due Capitola (Cappy) Bowse. Her endurance and unstinting commitment to her children, through decade after decade of troubled times, is an indelible tribute to women and mothers everywhere. The Author acknowledges his sister, Jo Baumgartner and his wife, Marilyn Zimmer as significant contributors to Cappy's Journal.

Thank you for choosing to read Cappy's Journal. If you liked this book, please leave a review! Your review is important to the author. For additional information regarding eclectic short-stories by Gary Leon Zimmer, please send your email address (and name) to: glzimm56@gmail.com

Cappy's Journal:

Part I

Capitola? Origin of her name and why?
Cappy: High School Only 1 of 7 siblings to graduate!
Roy Zimmer/Husband #I Michael Son #1 and Gary Son #2
Johnny 'Coug' Edmonson Husband #II Harvey Son #3
Alfred Baumgartner Husband #III Tony Son #4 Rick Son #5, Jo Daughter

Cappy's Journal:

Part II

Cappy's New Home/Evergreen Lodge
Yes, you're still my mother. . .
My Move in Party
Cappy's First Day at Evergreen Lodge
Cappy's Entry: Second Day
Journal: January 19th, 2004/May 14th, 2004
Life Care Center
Last Days

Cappy's Journal:

Part III

Short Biographies of Roy Zimmer's Children/Grandchildren

Cappy's Journal

This is the story of the last few months of the life of an eighty-nine year old woman as told by her son, Gary (Gib) Zimmer. You will delight in the verbal give and take between Cappy and her son as they discuss the serious and the whimsical aspects of life while Cappy is a resident of Evergreen Lodge, an assisted living center in Federal Way, Washington, just a few miles south of Seattle.

We introduce you to Cappy at fourteen (1931) and briefly describe the path that led to Evergreen Lodge seventy-five years later.

Part I

CAPITOLA ORLEE BOWSE

The Road to Evergreen Lodge

Cappy wanted to know *why?* Her siblings, from oldest brother Fred right down through Lois, Ida May, Earl, Vera and Glen, had normal names . . . and hers . . . Capitola? It didn't help at all that the 'i' was silent. The name was still a monster and teachers invariably mispronounced it!

Her mother, Roxanne, patiently explained, again and again that she was named after a character in a book Roxanne read just weeks before Cappy was born. Cappy silently wished her mother had read a book whose main character had been Jane, or Mary, or even Abigail . . . or Molly . . . but Capitola?

Cappy distributed blame between E.D. Southworth, the author of *Capitola's Peril*, and her mother, each conspiring with the other to sentence her to this life long ordeal of name correction and then the ensuing explanation of *why*.

Overwhelming to a fourteen year old!

But soon, Cappy would have no interest or time to dwell on the awkwardness of her given name. Cappy's goal was to be the first of her family to complete *high school!* In the midst of the country's worst depression ever, it meant helping her mother clean the homes of Lewiston, Idaho's elite every afternoon after school and then going home and studying for a couple of hours after dinner and before bed. Studying with five siblings still at home, three of them younger than Cappy, was going to require stamina and focus. Cappy was up to the task! With support from Roxanne and constant encouragement from her father, Earl Sr., and the help of a special teacher, Miss Vivian, Cappy sailed through the four years and earned the treasured diploma.

Good choices promised a bright future for Cappy. Two more years at Lewiston State Normal School and Cappy would be qualified to teach. But as happens with many young women, Cappy's well ordered future was altered by a bad choice.

LEROY ALBERT ZIMMER

Somehow, somewhere she met Roy Zimmer. Slender, blue eyes, a confident manner and an ability to use words one or two levels above anyone in a crowded room, Roy Zimmer was a charmer, easily attracting unsophisticated younger women who were barely more than girls. Cappy was captivated by the smooth talk, the warm smile and the mystery surrounding this older man. He didn't say much about his past and, with verbal agility, answered Cappy's direct questions with vague references to advanced education and family money.

Cappy was nineteen and Roy Zimmer was thirty-one when they were married in 1936. Prior to his marriage to Cappy, Roy Zimmer had been married to Mae Hiatt in 1929 and Beth Meleina Barry in 1932. Unknown to Cappy, Zimmer had been incarcerated at Washington State's McNeil Island Penetentiary in 1934 for violations of the nation's drug laws.

Cappy's father attempted to dissuade her, to no avail. The marriage was of short duration, just three years. Cappy's first two sons, Michael and Gary, would be borne of this union. Roy Zimmer would marry one more time in nineteen forty-six to Verla Mae Winslow. This marriage would be of even shorter duration, less than one year. Roy was forty and Verla Mae was eighteen. Roy Zimmer abandoned this young family before his daughter, Victoria Ann, was born. Victoria would never meet her father. (Sixty-six years later, due to intensive search by a genealogist, Victoria discovered the existence of an older half-brother, Gary Zimmer, living in Federal Way, Washington. Gary's brother, Michael Zimmer, also Victoria's half-brother, died in 1993.)

JOHNNY 'COUG' EDMONSON

Cappy should have listened to her father. Roy Zimmer deposited Cappy, now pregnant with Michael, with his brother Benjamin's family living in O'Neal, California. Michael was born in July of 1937. Roy was present for the birth of his first child, but as was typical of this itinerant fruit tramp, bartender, he soon set out, purportedly, to find work, leaving his young wife and new born child behind. He was gone for the next eleven months. He returned in July of 1938, stayed roughly one month and left again.

By this time Cappy had had enough of Roy Zimmer. Pregnant with Gary, Michael in tow, she returned to Lewiston and began divorce proceedings. On March 23rd, 1939, she gave birth to her second son, and, with help from Earl Bowse Sr., she rented a small house just a short distance from the home where she'd grown up on Clearwater Avenue. She took a job working as a waitress at a downtown restaurant.

Within the small confines of Lewiston there were now three daughters of Earl and Roxanne Bowse who were all single. Lois was the oldest, Cappy followed, then Vera.

Cappy would allow herself to be cajoled (if not coerced) into accompanying Vera and Lois to The Stables, a favorite night spot for Lewiston's young adults to frequent. Vera would remonstrate with Cappy for being one of the *undernourished* because she weighed a paltry one hundred-twenty pounds compared to the two hundred-fifty plus of her two sisters.

Vera met a young woman named Callie Edmonson at the Stables. Callie introduced Cappy to her brother, a handsome, well-muscled young logger, Johnny 'Coug' Edmonson. The 'Coug' was a shortened version of a ferocious feline's name and should have hinted at Johnny Edmonson's true character. But Cappy was young and not yet capable of acute discernment. And Coug Edmonson had not yet begun to abuse women and children. That would come later.

He was honest with Cappy. He told her he'd been married briefly and, like Cappy, he had two children, a daughter (name unknown) and a son named Jimmy. They lived in another state.

The young single mother and the just slightly older logger began to keep company. There were no objections to this burgeoning embryo of a romance because Johnny Edmonson seemed like a good match for Cappy. Her new beau came from a good family. Coug's mother and father were of Scandinavian descent; both gentle souls, and they embraced Cappy as one of their own.

Cappy's marital debacle with Roy Zimmer had made her cautious to the extreme. She was determined to maintain the moral standards of a single woman of her era. As the relationship progressed, Cappy found it necessary to keep Coug Edmonson at arm's length . . . that is until fate seemingly compelled her to make a decision, one she sensed was premature.

North Bonneville, Washington was a typical example of small town America. The town was cozied up against a large forested area on one side and the Columbia River on the other. Just a few hundred feet separated the grocery store, the movie theater, the Police Station and the town watering hole, The Bonneville Gardens. Right next to The Bonneville Gardens was the one room jailhouse (see picture below of Cappy and Mary, brother Glen's future wife. Just over Mary's right shoulder one can see the jailhouse.) And to the left of Cappy, easily seen, is the front of Bonneville Gardens. Those guilty of imbibing too much at the Gardens often found themselves temporarily housed in the jailhouse.

Cappy and Sister-in-law, Mary

Just a block and a half from the Main Street of North Bonneville was the Bonneville Dam, recently built to harness the raging waters of the Columbia River allowing for creation of power for the residents of the region. Just a couple of miles up the highway travelers came upon *The Bridge of the Gods,* a man made bridge connecting the Washington side to *Cascade Locks*, a small town on the Oregon side of the Columbia.

Coug Edmonson came to Cappy with excitement in his eyes telling her he'd been offered a logging job in the picturesque town of North Bonneville. He described North Bonneville as Mayberry would be described though Mayberry did not yet exist, even fictionally. "The business area of town is separated from the residential side by a patch of dense forest about a quarter of a mile across; the Columbia River is less than a five minute walk from the highway running through the town; there are multiple lakes for fishing and swimming within walking distance from the cluster of homes on North Bonneville's eastside residential area, there are hundreds of meadows and glades brimming with wild flowers."

Cappy knew what was coming and was immediately torn. It was too soon, she wasn't sure and, once again, if she accepted the proposal she knew was coming, it meant leaving Lewiston and the security of her parents and brothers and sisters. But her boys needed a father and Coug was a man's man, someone Mike and Gary could look up to and learn from. The thought of raising them in a Tom Sawyer like paradise appealed to Cappy. She was uncertain of her feelings for Coug Edmonson but she had to admit, she was strongly attracted to his stalwart presence. Life was a gamble, wasn't it?

And so it came to be. Cappy married for the second time and the newly formed family moved to the small town beside the Columbia River. Her decision to marry Coug Edmonson was not based on the man alone, but his almost poetic description of North Bonneville turned out to be providential. Dense forests within a mere hundred yards of the town boundaries, glacial lakes for fishing and swimming, and the embracing warmth of the people residing in the town of North Bonneville—it became home to Cappy and her boys. There was just one problem. She had married the wrong man . . . again . . . and had another child by this wrong man. Harvey, Cappy's third son was born August 9th, 1943.

HARVEY EDMONSON (SON #3)

Once away from the restraints of Cappy's family, Coug Edmonson's depiction of tenderness, caring and good manners, fell away and the successfully repressed violence of his true nature, surfaced. Without provocation he began to beat his wife and send his stepsons out to cut switches, switches he would then use to beat them with. Frequently the boys would return with switches deemed to be deficient in circumference and they would be sent to cut larger switches.

Coug Edmonson drank prodigious amounts but his consumption of alcohol had nothing to do with the brutality he unleashed on Cappy, Mike and Gib. Sober or drunk, whimsically it seemed, he would beat his wife and children.

Years went by. Cappy endured. Mike and Gib, young though they were, avoided going home except for sleep and an occasional meal. Their stepfather seemed to accept their absence, even embrace it. The boys spent time with Cappy's friends, Tex Eggleston and Peg Erickson, played with Butch and Alice, the Madsen children, and spent each summer with their Aunt Ida and Uncle Zeph in the central Washington city of Yakima.

Most of the citizens of North Bonneville thought it best to mind their own business. Domestic violence was viewed much differently in the nineteen-forties than it would be decades later. A man could beat his wife and punish his children anyway he chose without threat of repercussions. A man's home was his castle. When Cappy tried to leave him—Coug Edmonson threatened to kill her and his own child, Harvey.

Cappy was left to her own devices until late in 1946 when she became acquainted with Grandma Kaize, a neighbor from across the street. Grandma Kaize, a white-haired, wizened octogenarian, turned out to be Cappy's mentor and she could see right through to the cowardice of Coug Edmonson. She saw him as a bully, tough with women and children but without the courage to stand up to someone of equal physical stature.

Her son, Chuck Kaize, was not a resident of North Bonneville but he visited his mother frequently. Chuck, a gentle giant totally absent of malice and slow to anger, was capable of violence when he witnessed the abuse of women, children or animals. His mother, in casual conversation, made him aware of the beating of the young woman living in the small home next to the jailhouse just across the street from her. And the abuse of her children.

Chuck Kaize waited for an opportunity. When Edmonson took some extra money he'd put away and bought a beautiful roan stallion, the opportunity came.

When he saw Edmonson take a switch to the corralled horse and begin to beat it about the flanks, Chuck grabbed the front of Edmonson's shirt and slapped him several times, then easily pushed the smaller man to the ground. By this time, a few townspeople had gathered at the fence of the corral to see the wife beater, the bully who beat his children, get what was coming to him.

Coug regained his feet and took an awkward swing that Kaize easily sidestepped. He put Coug on the ground again with a short forceful jab to his jaw. Kaize said, "Think before you raise your hand to an animal, a child or a woman again!" More softly, "if I come back you'll wish you'd never been born!"

Coug could have gotten up but he chose not to. He wasn't contending with a woman or a child. This was not a battle he could win. North Bonneville's citizens rejoiced openly and collectively, all agreeing; it had been time for Coug Edmonson to 'pay the piper'.

After his beating by Chuck Kaize, Coug Edmonson stopped abusing his wife and stepchildren. However, he continued to threaten Cappy with his promise to kill her and Harvey if she tried to leave him. Her octogenarian friend from across the street, quietly mentored her regarding one simple fact of life . . . 'to ever live happily and in peace, one will eventually need courage.'

She advised Cappy to take her children and leave and Cappy took her advice.

Her leaving was uneventful. Cappy and the boys, Michael, Gib and baby Harvey, boarded a Greyhound and began the journey home to Lewiston and Cappy's family.

Once in Lewiston Cappy immediately filed for divorce. Then, after depositing Mike with her oldest sister Lois, (living in Pomeroy about 30 miles from Lewiston) and Gib with her father and mother, she left with Harvey for Hermiston, Oregon to spend a few months with her Aunt Edith, her father's sister. She wanted to be away from Lewiston avoiding any possibility of encountering Coug Edmonson prior to the divorce being final.

In Hermiston, Cappy went to work in what she called a hash house and would eventually teach her children all the unique terms used as shorthand for orders to the cook. Several months later, having saved enough money, she gathered Mike and Gib and moved to Yakima, Washington, where her sister Ida Mae Lizotte and husband Zeph provided a temporary place to stay until she was able to afford a home of her own. It was in Yakima where Cappy would meet her third husband, a non-violent but verbally abusive man named Al Baumgartner.

AL BAUMGARTNER

Cappy's first order of business when she arrived in Yakima was to find work. Shady Comers, a tavern at the corner of Fruitvale and Sixth Avenue, needed a waitress to serve the beer ordered by the Corners' customers. Alfred Baumgartner, a high energy charmer recently returned from the war, was an occasional customer at Shady Corners.

One of seven children born to Anton and Adelaide Baumgartner in North Dakota's farm country, young Alfred was just nine when Adelaide died in childbirth. The absence of a maternal guiding hand and a father who drank heavily while neglecting his farm, created a hardscrabble existence for the Baumgartner children.

As with most families in farming communities in and around Strasburg, North Dakota, only German was spoken at home and Alfred learned little English at school. He joined the U.S. Army in 1941. He was seventeen (his brother-in-law, John Feist filled out the enlistment form giving the teenager's age as one year older than he actually was) and America was at war.

Sixteen weeks of training followed. Then Baumgartner was sent to the Pacific zone where he was wounded. After a four week hospital stay fortune smiled upon the young soldier and he was sent to Australia. A relationship with a young Aussie girl resulted in her becoming pregnant just prior to Baumgartner receiving orders to return to the states. He left before his son was born. (The son born of this union was named Gary. Gary and his mother would eventually emigrate to Florida. Once established in Florida an attempt was made to initiate contact with Al Baumgartner. Ostensibly, the attempt was for medical reasons that might help Gary with any potential illness. Baumgartner chose not to meet with his son or provide medical records.)

Back in the states Corporal Al Baumgartner and some fellow soldiers, overcome with an occasion of indolence common to the rank and file, happened on a deuce and a half filled to the brim with whiskey. Over the following twenty-four hours these few soldiers became many and the truck was driven to an isolated location. After a couple of days the AWOL soldiers were discovered, punishment was meted out and Corporal Al Baumgartner was busted back to Private.

Shortly thereafter, in November of 1945, he was discharged. Finally, his war years done, civilian Al Baumgartner could go home. But home was no longer Strasburg, North Dakota. His destination upon discharge was the central Washington (State) city of Yakima, apple country, U.S.A. Two of his sisters, Christine and Elizabeth, and a brother Joe, had taken up residence in Yakima. Al went to work with Joe changing large industrial tires for General Tire.

It wasn't long before Al Baumgartner's path led him to Shady Corners where he immediately noticed the pert new server placing beers in front of customers with a smile.

Cappy, still young, still impressionable, was fully aware of the obstacles present in each day of life for a single woman with three children. But all of the economic and emotional challenges she would face as a mother raising three boys by herself became minor considerations. As love will, love happened. The couple was married on September 10th, 1950. Their first residence was 407 1/2 South First Street (The House in the Alley *by Gary Leon Zimmer*).

This troubled marriage was to last for 43 years. Cappy dealt with the former army corporal's verbal abuse every day of each of those forty-three years. When he was sober the threat of violence (though never delivered) was palpably present. If he was sleeping and could hear a voice coming from the kitchen or the living room he would pound on the wall and shout swear words in both German and English. He never smiled or made any attempt to make Cappy's children his friends, much less embrace them as a father.

Michael Zimmer (son #1)

Entering his teens, Mike needed the guidance and a gentle hand from Cappy's new husband. What he received was a cacophony of constant verbal abuse. The die was cast. An iron-willed teenager against a militant, iron-fisted former U.S. Army NCO; an expletive spewing tyrant whose very manhood was challenged by a young boy, devoid of any power. A boy who couldn't put a roof over his head, couldn't feed himself, and did not yet have the muscle to stand up to the former corporal. An unfair contest.

Mike was lost. He'd gone from the physically abusive Coug Edmonson to the unceasing tension and the constant threat of violence his new stepfather promised for even a slight misstep from his oldest stepson. Not a follower, Mike was a leader. With that gentle hand, the guidance of a caring male figure, he would have become less belligerent, more malleable, and he would have developed a sense of humor. Whip-smart but lacking that guiding hand, Mike Zimmer began looking for the easy way to get along, much like the way of life chosen by his biological father, the man who had abandoned him.

He began to cut school, stay out for two or three nights running, steal and lie. Out of control, petty crimes followed. Police intervened and eventually he was sent to Green Hill Academy, a resident program for delinquent boys.

On his release from Green Hill, Mike, fourteen, would spend his time at the homes of friends or in Lewiston with relatives, anywhere but at his own home in Yakima. He was a tough guy, tall, rail thin and he presented an ominous physical presence. Working for a living was for the other guy and Mike, in the fifty-six years he lived, would never hold a real job. There was something else he would never do. He would never bend. He was always right. And while he would never start a fight, he would never turn his back on one.

Cappy saw the impact her new husband had on her three boys. She considered leaving him but it would mean returning to the hand to mouth existence she was leading prior to her new marriage. Her two younger sons were different than the steely-willed Mike. Second eldest, Gib to his family, was a peacemaker, not the least confrontational, wanting everyone to get along. He went to whatever lengths he could to make things easier for his mother. Harvey the youngest, was gifted in his ability to make everyone around him love him, but Harvey was slow and never learned to read or write beyond a few words. Cappy's hands were full and she decided to stay with the volatile Al Baumgartner. Additionally, she was pregnant with Tony, his birth just a few months distant.

Cappy would eventually have three children with Al Baumgartner. They shared the same experience of their older stepbrothers. Baumgartner worked hard, provided food for his family, but his paternal behavior was consistent with all six children except Mike; distance, constant yelling, binges from Friday night into the early hours of Sunday morning.

Al traded cars often. He usually lost a couple hundred dollars to each practiced salesman who saw the gleam in his eye when looking at the gorgeous blue of a 52 Chevy convertible coupe with the unseen oil leak slowly darkening the dirt flooring of Ralph or Harry's Used Cars. One year stretched into another as Cappy found ways to make her family more economically stable, and eventually, with the help of her sister Ida May and brother-in-law Zeph, she was able to buy a two-story fixer-upper on Yakima's west side. The home on Fairbanks Avenue would be Cappy's home for the next forty-five years.

For twenty-seven of those years, Al Baumgartner worked hard and drank heavily while his step children became adults and moved out to fend for themselves. Then, eventually, his biological children also left school and began their own lives. Cappy, never much of a drinker, followed her husband around as he became a pronounced alcoholic until, one day, his ability to keep it all together began to fail him. A couple of DUI's resulted in heavy fines and enhanced insurance costs. His speech, always broken because of the German he spoke throughout his childhood, became increasingly hard to understand after further being compromised by alcohol.

Cappy began making the choice to remain home rather than suffer the inevitable embarrassment resulting from Al's excessive drinking.

In Cappy's absence her husband's watering holes of choice changed to just one watering hole. He no longer patronized the Lewisville Tavern, the Ranch Tavern and the Little Dutch Inn. His patronage became exclusive to the Veteran's of Foreign Wars Hall. At the VFW Hall, Cappy's companionship was replaced by a woman named Ruth, a class act with an abundance of Safeway stock. Widowed, Ruth was unaware of the construction worker's marital status. The first hours of every evening she spent with him were pleasant but ultimately, after several drinks, his speech became garbled and his sentences unintelligible. She would walk away, but the next time he walked through the door, she would be there waiting, with a smile.

As this was happening, Cappy began to yearn for peace and quiet at home instead of the pandemonium created when he drank and the ensuing silence as he sobered up. Tolerance had given way to dread. Cappy asked him to move out and he did. To the driveway, to a small trailer sitting there, a trailer he'd pulled to construction sites when working out of town. Both Cappy and Al were ready for change. She had retired from packing fruit at Pacific Fruit and Produce and began to collect Social Security. The house was paid for and she'd saved some money. Her kids would be there for her. And soon, Al Baumgartner would have a cathartic three day experience that would alter the rest of his life, and make him amenable to his new love interest. However, those three days would be the worst three days of his life.

After an especially severe drinking bout, the man capable of charming the outside world while punishing everyone he lived with, the ex soldier, the Herculean drinker, at sixty-two—got the DT's in his trailer. Imagined snakes and spiders crawled all over him covering him and creating unbearable horror and, to make things worse, he was physically incapable of getting up from the trailer floor. Once the snakes and spiders had gone to wherever imaginary snakes and spiders go, Al Baumgartner still could not get up off the trailer floor. Help was just steps away. Cappy was in the house and would have come to his rescue, but allowing him to live within the trailer parked in what she considered her driveway, was as far as she would go in making his life comfortable. There was no way she was going to be checking to see if he was all right.

Conscious at times, unconscious at other times, having the DTs at times and then simply lying there and wondering when they would return, incapable of standing, eating or going to the bathroom to relieve himself for three days, he experienced a living Hell. Eventually the poisonous venom eked out of his pores. Eventually, in tiny increments, his strength returned and he was able to stand. And clean up.

Al Baumgartner would never drink again. It was over for him and to his credit, in the next two months, he lost weight and quit smoking. He had a new lease on life and, ultimately, a new woman in his life. He returned to the VFW Hall for just one reason, to collect Ruth. Now that the volatile German was whole he was ready to begin his life with a new partner.

Cappy was not upset. She had full command of her life. She loved her home and all of her children were attentive and visited often. She gardened, made friends with the neighborhood children, all of whom called her 'Nana', drank coffee at her kitchen table and spent much of her day watching the school children frolicking at Garfield Elementary School's playground directly across the street from her home.

And she could look out at her driveway and feel total relief at the empty space formerly occupied by Al Baumgartner's trailer. He was in Arizona with Ruth. Cappy was happy for both of them. Although the years of raising her children in the house on Fairbanks were good years, the presence of tension and immense stress, on a daily basis, had made living there almost unbearable.

The following twenty-two years were free of the fear of awakening the physical form of torment, sleeping one wall away. Finally, most of her work done, peace and tranquility had entered Cappy's life.

It was her time!

Part II

CAPPY'S NEW HOME/EVERGREEN LODGE

Capitola 'Cappy' Bowse was born in 1916. Her mother named her after a young heroine from the novel 'The Hidden Hand' written by E.D.E.N. Southworth, a popular nineteenth century writer.

Upon graduating from high school in Lewiston, Idaho, she married an itinerant fruit picker named Roy Zimmer and had two sons, Gary and Michael. After this marriage foundered, Cappy married a logger named Johnny 'Coug' Edmonson and had a third son, Harvey in 1943.

Once again her marriage failed. She moved with her three sons to Yakima, Washington, where she met her third and final husband, Alfred Baumgartner. Her last three children, Anton, Richard and Jo Ann were born of this union. Cappy and Alfred were married for forty-three years and then divorced.

Early 2003 brought changes. Cappy's mobility had declined and she began to experience frequent memory lapses. Except for monthly visits from Gary (Gib to his family) and his wife Marilyn and daughter Jo, Cappy had little contact with people. Small things like getting to the grocery store and putting her garbage cans out for collection had become problematical.

Cappy's children decided she could no longer live alone safely. Jo, living in a large rented home in Auburn just southeast of Seattle, suggested her mother occupy a couple of unused rooms in her home, with total access to living room, TV room and a large kitchen. Cappy agreed and a month later the move was accomplished.

All was well for a short time. Then the day came when she missed a step while descending from the kitchen into the sunken living room. She broke three ribs and began to experience respiratory problems. When her breathing difficulties continued, Cappy was taken to Auburn Northwest Hospital where she was diagnosed with pneumonia. After three days of continued improvement, doctors informed her family that she was ready to leave the hospital, but cautioned, she would need both rehabilitation and twenty-four hour medical supervision.

Just outside the entrance to the hospital, Jo, Gib and his wife, Marilyn, and Jason, Cappy's grandson, looked over the list of nursing homes given to them by the hospital staff. A woman, standing just a few feet away, overheard the discussion and suggested a nursing home and rehabilitation center in the nearby community of Puyallup. Life Center of Puyallup had given her father excellent care.

A call to this facility determined that a bed was not immediately available. A staff member suggested a sister facility in Auburn. Cappy was a resident at LC of Auburn for just one week before transferring to the more spacious circumstances of LC of Puyallup. A good diet, a caring staff and a daily regimen of exercise, created a healthy and fit Cappy in just thirty days.

The professionals at Life Center suggested Cappy would be an ideal candidate for an assisted living situation. Marilyn and Gib visited just two assisted living centers before discovering the idyllic Evergreen Lodge in their city of Federal Way. They were impressed with the upbeat residents, the polite and smiling staff and the facility's director, Luuk, who spent a couple of hours each Friday evening entertaining his residents with his lively renditions of Folk classics.

Evergreen Lodge is just a stone's throw from Seattle. Cappy is happily ensconced there and enjoys the privacy of her own apartment, three meals served restaurant style each day, and a beautiful view of Mt. Rainier from her window.

Jo lives close to Evergreen Lodge as does Gib and Harvey. They see her several times a week. Tony and Rick, Cappy's younger sons, live in Yakima, the eastern Washington city where she'd made her home for fifty-five years. Cappy's eldest son, Michael passed away in 1993 from complications of diabetes and emphysema.

Gib wrote the following description of Cappy's first days at Evergreen Lodge.

Cappy's Journal follows this description.

<u>Gib</u> (Gary Zimmer son #2)

<u>Yes, you're still my mother</u>

She emerged unsteadily from my sister Jo's Lincoln. My wife and I watched from inside the door at Evergreen Lodge, the assisted living center chosen to be my mother's new home. Our role was to make mom feel welcome and comfortable in her new surroundings. No small task, as we were to learn shortly.

When I saw how unsteady she was, I approached and gently took her left arm. Seeing me, she broke into a big smile and said, 'Gib, what are you doing here?' We've always had this great rapport. She understands my 'funny side' and laughs heartily, knowing full well when I'm poking fun at the world, myself, even her, while the humor often eludes everyone else. But this was an occasion for candor, not humor.

"I'm here to welcome you to your new home!"

"I don't live here!" she replied.

Mom is eighty-eight and her favorite line is, "Don't remember!" She is sincere when she makes this statement even though, at times, a simple mental effort and she would remember. Since, singularly or collectively, we could not be with her 24 hours a day, her doctors advised that her circumstances would be ideal for an assisted living situation. But she forgets, hence the, 'I don't live here' declaration.

We entered the building and made our way to the elevator. Once on the second floor we easily found room 261. Once inside the room she took everything in. She saw her blue recliner, her soft brown suede love seat and her television set. She walked to the window and looked out at an incredible view of Mount Rainier. Then she turned and confronted us.

"You'll visit every day?"

"Yes, one of us will be here every day."

"You won't forget where I am?"

We assured her 'we would always know where she is' and visit every day!

During one such visit recently she described the detachable windows on the touring car her father used to transplant his family from South Dakota to Lewiston, Idaho seventy-five years ago. When this description ended, we asked her what she had been served for lunch and she said, 'Don't remember'.

We write the details of our visits in a tablet so she'll know we've been to see her. Seeing an entry from my sister in the tablet an hour and forty-five minutes before I had come to visit, I said, 'So, Jo was here a little while ago.'

She replied, 'No, I haven't seen her.' I gently explain how I know her daughter had visited.

She laughed and said, "I'm still your mother!"

I asked what she meant and she said, laughing again, 'Even if I get 'screwier', I'm still your mother.'

On this earth or wherever you might be, you're still my mother . . .

Cappy's Journal:
My Move in Party

Ryan and Cappy (Jo's son, Cappy's grandson)

Cappy: My grandson Ryan, Jo's son, and his wife Lisa are here for my move in party. Gib and Marilyn as well. They tell me my new home is called Evergreen Lodge and they assure me that I'm going to like it here. My studio apartment is small but more than comfortable. All of my furniture is here and I have a beautiful view of Mt. Rainier. I know my memory isn't good and I'm already unsure of how I got here. I'm afraid all of them, Gib, Marilyn, Jo, Ryan and Lisa, will forget where I am.

Cappy's First Day At Evergreen Lodge:

Jo, Ryan and Lisa leave. Marilyn and Gib escort Cappy to the all-purpose room where some of the residents are sitting in comfortable chairs reading or watching John Wayne and Montgomery Clift in 'Red River'. Cappy says she likes the room. She is immediately mesmerized by the colorful fish of different sizes darting fluidly throughout a large fish tank.

Residents smile and say 'hello' to Cappy, the newcomer. Cappy responds with, "This is my son Gib and my daughter-in-law, Marilyn." In the months to come she would introduce me to these same people over and over again. These gracious and polite people would smile and say ' hello' as if meeting me for the first time each new time we met.

Cappy becomes restless after a while and asks, "Can I go home now."

I reply "Mom, you are home."

Repeating the same words she'd stated earlier, Cappy says, "I don't live here."

I say "Mom, this is your new home. You have your own studio apartment, three meals a day served restaurant style and staff people to take care of your every need."

Her surprise was genuine even though we had just left room 261 a few minutes earlier.

"I have an apartment right here in this building?"

I smile at her and wink. "No, mom, to get home you have to leave the building, catch a bus, stay on the bus for three miles . . . then get out and hitchhike for another three miles . . . "

She laughs as I knew she would. "I'm not hitchhiking anywhere. You say I live here? Then show me where. I want to take a nap."

Leaving the all-purpose room we make one turn and in just a few steps we're in front of the elevator. Up one floor and one more turn and we're in front of room 261. Cappy is ready to spend her first night at Evergreen Lodge.

"You'll be back tomorrow?"

"We'll be back tomorrow."

"You won't forget where I am?"

"Mom, we'll always know where you are."

Jo Baumgartner (Child #6, Cappy's daughter)

CAPPY'S ENTRY SECOND DAY

Gib visited me today. Jo left a note asking him to call Quest and get my phone hooked up. I had to laugh at him. He immediately picked up the phone's receiver and attempted to call Quest. He was surprised when he didn't get a dial tone. And they tell me I'm the one who needs help getting through the day?

Gib: Second day: So I tried to call the phone company using the same dead line I would like them to activate. She said something about the blind leading the blind and suggested I spend a few minutes appreciating the pristine beauty of Mt. Rainier. "It might help clear your head!"

She is sharp, good with words and her sense of humor seems to become more acute each day.

Mom is using her cane to get around and seems to be moving fairly well. She isn't so concerned about people forgetting her today. Is Cappy getting her thyroid pills? I'll check with the nurse's station downstairs.

What are we going to do about Fannie, mom's dog? All of us agree, a large debt is owed to Fannie for the loyalty and companionship she provided Cappy in the final eleven years they shared the Fairbanks house. Evergreen Lodge permits pets but Cappy is on the second floor. And she doesn't possess the mobility required to get Fannie outside two or three times a day. What to do? What to do?

January 19th, 2004
Gib arrived at 3:30 p.m. Cappy expressed fear of the future or, a better way to put it, the potential brevity of her future.

I reminded her, "You've already beaten the odds by living way beyond the average." We discussed the possibility I might precede her in that direction . . . as one of her sons already has.

She doubts that I will but, we agreed, there are no guarantees.

I suggested her love affair with her bed and the immense comfort these four walls seem to provide her, hint at a readiness for God to appear and say . . . 'Cappy, come with me' and her admonition to the great one . . . 'Ok, but go slow so I can keep up . . .'

January 20th, 2004
Jo visiting. I made mom change her pajamas. She resisted but I'm going to win this battle every time. She called me a bossy lil' gal and wouldn't talk to me for a while.

Please don't give her hard candy. She falls asleep and chokes on it!

January 21st, 2004
Cappy is apprehensive about her living circumstances here at Evergreen Lodge. She asks, "Will I be able to find my apartment after meals? Will I be able to find the elevator?"

She is concerned about her ability to remember the names of her neighbors after meeting them. All are valid concerns reminiscent of that first day at school. We reassure her gently, repeatedly.

January 22nd, 2004
Fannie, Cappy's canine companion for many years, has a new home! Fannie will live right here at Evergreen Lodge with Judy, a friendly and outgoing ground floor resident. This is a great solution to the Fannie problem. Cappy will see Fannie on a frequent basis and Judy, who has always wanted a pet but has been unable to afford the twenty-five dollar monthly fee required of residents who own pets, will be Fannie's new owner. Cappy's family will pay all expenses. Doing so will help repay Fannie for her years of loyalty to Cappy! And we'll continue to witness the wonderful enthusiasm Fannie displays each time she sees a familiar face.

Unfamiliar faces? Another story! As is her troubled relationship with the U.S. Postal Service! More about that later.

January 23rd, 2004
Cappy is complaining of loneliness. We continually encourage her to go downstairs and visit with some of the other residents. She states, 'They don't know me.'

I say, "What about the banner covering one wall of the TV room asking . . . Where Is Cappy?"

She says, "God, I hope you're kidding!" I reply, "Yes, I'm kidding, but if you wait too long to introduce yourself I'm going to help them paint it!"

I tried to put some cold water in her pitcher last night and discovered one gets *hot* water from one spigot and *warm* water from the other. I let the nurse downstairs know 'there is no cold water.' She said she would inform maintenance. I haven't checked today as of yet but I will. Internet service is working. Just about time for dinner.

January 24th, 2004
Marilyn, Gib and Cappy went to IHOP for lunch. And what a lunch it was. Steven was our waiter. Mom had a hamburger (dry, uck) . . .

She wore my sunglasses throughout the meal (incognito, aged movie star). Jo did a good job of purchasing clothes for mom. Marilyn and I especially like the 'Happy' shirt, since, with Cappy in it, she becomes 'Happy Cappy'.

While eating, Marilyn related a couple of her veterinary assistant stories . . . the man who brought his dog in because one hind leg had gone lame. It turns out the dog's leg was caught in his collar which Marilyn discovered readily . . . also the woman who attempted to remove 'ticks' from the stomach of her puppy making the belly of the young dog raw . . . only to be told by the Vet 'the ticks are in actuality the dog's nipples!' "But," the woman said, "The dog is male!" "Doesn't your husband have nipples?" asked the Vet? Hmmm . . . idiot is a harsh term but . . .

January 25th, 2004
Marilyn visited while Gib spent time with his favorite dentist! The dentist loves his job . . . he gets to hurt people and dispense drugs without getting arrested!

All is well here except for a massive line of treelike bushes growing along the view side of the building. Don't know what they're called, but each twenty-four hours represents another two inch growth spurt. In a couple of weeks Cappy won't be able to see anything but the leaves of this burgeoning jungle. She isn't happy. I'll speak with Luuk and see what can be done.

January 26th, 2004
Mom is eating lunch downstairs. I'm waiting for the Comcast Installation Expert. We have to remember to cancel her service in 3 months . . . they will then take the box out but she'll still have access to ballgames and some other channels. I'm still waiting for papers from the City to sign her up for the 30% discount.

Comcast man is here and has hooked up the box but is not getting a signal . . . went out to check something.

Installation complete! Cappy can't get over how good the reception is. Mission accomplished!

January 27th, 2004
Gib and Marilyn visited. Mom is in the hallway with a couple of the other residents on her floor. One of the women mom is visiting with just moved into an apartment on the 2nd floor. Maybe she'll begin to make some friends after all . . .

January 28th, 2004
Mom asked, 'Do they notify us when it's time to eat?' I explained that Evergreen Lodge would get bad publicity if some of their residents expired due to malnutrition . . . the facility's positive PR was dependent on healthy residents and healthy residents were dependent on regular meals. Evergreen staff notifies residents of meals being served by knocking on each door and announcing that a meal is *about to be served* in the dining room. If a resident doesn't appear a staff member checks to see if they are Ok.

Cappy approved of the system.

No action on the tree to this date. I don't want to become the Evergreen *nag* and have them cringe every time I walk through the door. I noticed a landscape guy on the grounds. I'll mention it to him if he's still around when I leave.

January 29th, 2004
Gib and Marilyn visited. Arrived about 7:45. Mom is sitting up on the bed, alert, but not reading or watching television.

She has no towels in her bathroom, the cold water runs hot and the tree obscures her view of the mountain. All aside, they are very good to her here and I imagine these problems will be solved sometime soon.

Many years ago Cappy put her home on Fairbanks in Yakima in trust to her six children. Now the house sits empty and is quickly becoming uninhabitable. Jo and I are in agreement, something needs to be done about the house. Any decision regarding the house will involve all of Cappy's surviving five children. Can all of us agree on a solution?

January 30th, 2004
Each day I arrive at Evergreen Lodge my sole intent is to visit with my elderly mother. Occasionally, my ascent to room 261 is interrupted, almost always pleasantly, by one of the many residents I pass on my journey between entrance and elevator.

On this day, a slender octogenarian with a leathery, lined face is sitting in a chair next to the elevator. She is perusing a segment of a newspaper as I approach.

She looks up as I push the top button and asks, "Do you know where you're going?"

Can this wizened woman, the weight of her advanced years obvious from head to toe, see into the rampant confusion of my mind? Or, does she simply want to be helpful if I'm unsure of my direction?

I answer as accurately as possible, smiling, "Sometimes."

She laughs and says, "This building is so big I get lost all the time."

So I relax. My mental disarray is safe. I smile. "Second floor to visit Cappy, one of your neighbors."

Without further comment she returns to her newspaper.

I disappear into the elevator thinking of the corners, corridors, streets, countless cities, even different countries . . . but we sort them out and find our way. Then a time comes when a single building, known and familiar one day, becomes a hopeless maze the next. The arrogance of youth is ultimately tempered by the humility of the aging process.

January 31st, 2004
Cappy's granddaughter, Kari, visited her on this last Saturday in January. Kari is a paralegal for the City of Olympia, forty miles south of Evergreen Lodge. She visits her 'Nana' whenever

she can. They spent a couple of hours catching up on things before Kari took her leave.

Kari, nice granddaughter that she is, left a check to pay for Cappy's next two visits to Evergreen Lodge's own hair stylist, Carol.

February 1st, 2004
Cappy is on the bed resting when Gib and Marilyn arrive. Seems Santa has made a late delivery. New clothes for Cappy apparently purchased by Jo. So now Cappy can adhere to the two w's, whim and weather.

Cappy and I spent some time talking about her number three son, Harvey, and his ability to stay behind the veil, living a secret existence only he and the CIA fully understand.

Did the bulletin board fall down?

February 2nd, 2004
Gib dropped in (resounding thud) and watched two taped episodes of Becker with mom. Good show! She seemed to enjoy both. Brought her Hershey bars but not much interest as yet. Probably still full from dinner. We have talked separately to Luuk, Lisa, another staff person and, finally, George, the landscape guy, about mom's view being obstructed by the burgeoning treelike bush continuing to demand that all of us appreciate its puny leaves instead of the majestic view of Mt. Rainier. This ever flourishing monster of a bush blocks a bit more of the view each day. We have been promised action . . . we'll see.

I talked to a staff person in the dining room and she said Cappy does appear for most meals but doesn't eat much!

February 3rd, 2004
Fannie has a growth just above her right eye. It appears to be rubbing against the eye itself and needs to be removed. Are there enough funds in mom's account for this operation? We'll speak with Jo, the keeper of the purse! Regardless of the availability of Cappy's funds, the growth will be removed. We

just have to decide whether Bank of America or Wells Fargo is most vulnerable to masked bandits desperate for Vet dollars, about three hundred of them.

February 4th, 2004
The view blockage persists. Cappy is unhappy and threatening extreme and dangerous individual pursuit of a solution.

I'll talk to Luuk about the potential negative publicity of having a TV camera crew record the efforts of one of his elderly residents attempting to climb the offending tree with pruning shears locked between her teeth.

Could be the beginning of Cappy's ascent to aggressive activism!

February 5th, 2004
(Jo)

Just got here. Fannie's eye is expensive but she's worth it! Mom has the money so no problem there.

A decision has been made about the empty house on Fairbanks Avenue in Yakima. Cappy's grandson Jason will move into the house with his young family and pay a monthly rental of $250 a month. The plan is for Jason and his wife Kim, while paying this minimal rental amount, to save money for a down payment on a house of their own, and also allowing Cappy to pay some of her expenses with the rental income.

February 6th, 2004
Guess what? The tree has been trimmed (a little) and Cappy can now see all of the Albertson's parking lot and the street beyond! In two weeks the tree will be obscuring the view again, and we can start the ordeal of getting them to trim it all over again. I'm thinking of trying to find a helicopter firm willing to dispatch one of their flying machines to lower itself (upside down, blades down) to the bush and trim it to ground level; could be a bit dangerous for the copter.

Maybe a small maneuverable one like the Jetsons use would work?

Let's count our blessings! We have visual evidence! The mountain still exists.

February 7th, 2004
Gib & Marilyn visited Cappy this afternoon. She was exiting the bathroom when we arrived. Asked how she was doing she replied, "Ok, under the circumstances." What circumstances? "Being here alone all the time." Well, you don't have to be alone. "I know, there is a community downstairs."

Yes, there is . . .

February 8th, 2004
Mom has decided to meet God sooner than she would normally have to, by not eating! She confesses to eating just small amounts when she descends for her meals. I said, and she agreed, 'you have to eat to live'!

We visited for a while and, as often happens in a building with furniture being moved in and out, we heard a loud *thump* and mom asked, 'What was that?'

I said, "That was another Evergreen resident who decided *not to* eat!"

February 9th, 2004
Gib visited. Mom wants candy, hard candy! I told her I couldn't buy her hard candy.

She asked, "Why not?"

"Jo says you fall asleep and choke on it!"

"Jo's crazy", she replies.

"Can I tell her you said that?"

"Better not!" she says. Good decision . . .

I went downstairs to buy her a candy bar with the last dollar I had in my wallet. The candy machine took the dollar and gave me change. But no candy bar. I noticed a sign on the machine saying *use at your own risk*. So much for kindness to the elderly!

So, I returned to the room empty handed, a mom failure. But, her birthday being the following day, I assured her 'I will return tomorrow bearing gifts.'

February 10, 2004
I have two problems on this day. First, this happens to be Cappy's birthday. Secondly, I returned without the promised candy. Do you think she remembers today is her birthday? No, she doesn't. Do you think she remembers my promise to bring her some candy?

"Where is my candy?" she asks

The selectivity of her memory is amazing and I tell her so!

Her reply, "Where is my candy?" My ace in the hole? Marilyn is at the mall, now called 'The Commons', to pick up a birthday gift and candy.

"Marilyn is bringing your candy."

Her look said, "Marilyn is a princess and you owe her your life!" Then she smiled so she still loves me, but doesn't think I'm very reliable.

Asked mom how old she is now and she said '16'. Asked her when she was going to be '17'? 'Next year' she said. Mom's one remaining sibling, her brother Earl, still a resident of Lewiston, Idaho, after all these years, sent an email wishing his beloved sister a 'Happy Birthday'! His frequent emails, usually accompanied by a hilarious joke, always lighten our day.

Mom asks, "Will he stop sending them because we never send him one in return?" I assure her, I answer each one of his emails with lengthy replies. Some of them as lengthy as a short novel. Well, slight exaggeration.

Eventually, Marilyn arrives with goodies!

Rick and Tony called to wish Cappy a Happy Birthday! I am immeasurably pleased with my brothers! They came through for mom on her birthday!

Jo

Jo brought mom a huge piece of chocolate cake and she enjoyed every bite! Well, there's another piece so she'll enjoy more tomorrow. Gave her a black soft pants suit that actually fits! Stayed until midnight then went home to work some more.

A great day for this weathered and wizened octogenarian made even better when Jo stopped by in the evening with two large pieces of chocolate cake, one for Cappy's birthday and another (to be eaten the next day) as an apology for being a 'bossy lil' gal'. Jo may be a bit forceful but she knows how to negotiate forgiveness.

February 11th, 2004

Fannie and I visited the Vet while Judy made a trip to Seattle with her daughter. The operation to remove the cancerous growth from above her right eye would be a simple one, according to the vet. The removal should resolve the problem permanently.

Fannie's operation will cost around $190 plus antibiotics. We need to get her some Advantage. Cost? Roughly $45. Shots too!

The operation is scheduled for next Friday at roughly 10:00 a.m. Fannie will be kept there until around 5 p.m. With everything, sedation, surgery and a blood check to determine Fannie is otherwise healthy, plus yesterday's office visit, the bill will be around $300.

Fannie has gained some weight! In her younger days she could leap a good three feet into the air from a standstill. No longer. She gathered herself for the leap into the car, pushed off on all four feet, sailed upward and fell short of the seat by a good six inches. She looked back at me and her expression seemed one of embarrassment. But when she saw the smug look on my face the embarrassment was quickly replaced by disdain, as if to say, "Hey, Casper Longtooth, let's see you try it." Don't think so . . .

February 12th, 2004
Cappy continues to ask about her two sons still living in Yakima. We tell her they're doing fine and give her any news we've heard from the other side of the mountain, news usually coming to us by way of the occasional email or phone call from her grandson, Jason.

She says, "They probably don't know where I am."

I reassure her. "They know where you are."

She says, "Well, they're busy. Everyone's busy these days!"

I agree, saying, "Yes, mom, they're busy. When they have time they'll come and see you." And if the mountain remains in the distance, aloof and insensitive to the sunshine and joy of this wonderfully caring woman, she will, with her slow but constant gait, hobble laboriously, inexorably, toward the *mountain*.

February 13th, 2004
Fannie's operation was successful! The growth was removed, shots administered and Advantage purchased. Also, a full exam assured us of a healthy (if aging) canine. Hopefully, both Fannie and Cappy will endure for years. A well spent three hundred dollars.

Fannie was somewhat famous in Yakima for her war with the U.S. Postal system. She considered herself victorious in this limited conflict since the enemy discontinued visits to the home of her mistress. Strangely, just after the intruders stopped appearing, Cappy began to imprison her in a bedroom at the rear of the house for an hour every day of the week except one. Most dogs are rewarded for heroism! Humans are strange.

Judy informs me Fannie the Valiant, is challenging all who enter what she considers to be her domain. In this case *her domain* means Judy's apartment. All is well as long as Judy is in the apartment but, if a staff person enters to pick up laundry or for any other reason, Fannie becomes aggressive. On one occasion this friendly, tail wagging, human loving pooch actually nipped one of the staff. Skin was not broken but there was a red mark left from Fannie's teeth.

We talked about it. Fannie is just being territorial, something simply natural to her. However, another incident will force us to consider both the risk taken by those who are exposed to her and the issue of potential liability. To put an exclamation point on Fannie's aggression, she barked and growled when a staff member brought some medicine in for Cappy while Judy and I were visiting.

Judy said she would keep us informed!

February 14th, 2004
Valentine's Day! Otherwise known as *the abyss awaiting all who are genetically challenged in the romance department.* I buy the flowers and a gift not out of romanticism but, instead, self-preservation.

Any occasion delivering a large Hershey bar into Cappy's hands is a good occasion in her view! Flowers for her too! But Cappy, like her number two son, grew up with a practical bent, 'if it isn't functional why waste money on it?'

My only emotional link to the word Valentine is having known one so named as a teenager. He was of Latin background and I used an ill chosen term to describe his heritage one evening while my brain was disengaged. I apologized immediately and he simply said, 'forget it'. We remained friends but now, fifty years later, the memory still causes me pain.

Mom, in her earlier years, believed, in the interests of the children, blacks should marry blacks. I asked then, 'If I were a child of mixed parentage living down the block a little ways, would I be welcome in your home?' 'Of course you would . . . '

Hmmmm . . .

She states that she is not racial. She can see into the heart! If it is a good one she is unconcerned about the packaging.

In keeping with the theme of this entry, my friend John Brown, who is black, told me a joke the other day...

"What do you call a black man who flies an airplane?"

Hmmmm . . . a mine field. Beware! "I don't know", I answered truthfully.

"A pilot, you racist jerk!"

Yes, and why not . . .

February 15th, 2004
Came over to see mom Sunday evening and Jo was here. She had been here most of the day Saturday and virtually all day Sunday. We discussed the house on Fairbanks and lack of income for Cappy, income she needs to pay her phone bills, cable bills, Fannie bills, hair fixing bills, and the list goes on.

Jason has yet to pay rent for either January or February. I'm going to send off her phone bill and Cappy will reimburse the Zimmer's upon becoming wealthy again.

We love Jason but things are getting difficult financially. Maybe the time has come to sell the house?

Discovered that mom's discount for her cable will have to come through the City of Federal Way. In the process. Baseball season is approaching. Must get her cable set up. Cappy is a Mariners fan!

February 16th, 2004
I arrived here about 3:30 p.m. Mom is watching a 'Cheech and Chong' movie. She is demanding some of that 'stuff' creating so much frivolity in the movie. I remember visiting a relative on McNeil Island back in the seventies and being asked to bring him some of that 'stuff'. Now mom is asking me to smuggle a joint or two into Evergreen Lodge so she can toke up and wear her T-shirt that says, appropriately on the front, 'Happy Cappy' . . .

Ok, I made it up. So what? She might've suggested it . . . it's possible . . . right? . . . now I feel bad . . .

February 17th, 2004
Gib visited. Mom wearing blue sweatshirt and sweat pants. Gib said the sweatpants would disappear soon.

Mom asks, "Why?"

Gib answers, "A Classy woman like you loses just a bit of her class when she wears sweatpants!"

Mom says she has nothing else to wear.

She has some attractive outfits in her closet. I show her a couple of them after which I begin to feel guilty for imposing my standards on her. She has every right to wear what is comfortable in her own home.

I am ashamed and promise to do better!

Number three son, Harvey has surfaced . . . after thirteen years. Wants my help in getting a gold ring and a Rolex watch out of hock. Claims they are collectively worth over six thousand dollars. He needs six hundred and sixty dollars to retrieve them from hostage. I agreed to loan him the money if he would agree to leave the jewelry in my care until the loan is repaid.

"Not a problem", he says. (Just a short distance down the road a problem arises, then another, and another, partially due to circumstances, partially due to my weakness and being stupid, stupid, stu . . . well, point made.)

February 18th, 2004
Gib visited and found Cappy sitting in the hallway chatting with Velma. Velma lives in a ground floor unit right next to the elevator and can usually be seen sitting in a chair just outside her door. She suggested I take a 'load off' and join the conversation.

Ahhh, chance to help mom make a friend. Actually, she was doing quite well without my help.

I discovered that Velma spent some years in Mabton, Washington, the boyhood home of Mel Stottlemyre, a former pitching coach for the New York Yankees. Velma also lived in Selah, just outside of Yakima for a while.

After a few minutes we said goodbye to Velma and I escorted mom back to her room.

The sun is coming out so maybe mom will be able to see the mountain later. We talked about her meeting people downstairs and then not 'remembering them'. I told her 'meeting her neighbors over and over again will allow her to remember.' She talked about working in Yakima and having good kids, kids she adored. She says she now has grandchildren she doesn't see. We'll attempt to change that.

February 19th, 2004
Gib here at 5:30. Must leave by 6:15 for annual meeting at Habitat. Mom just returned from dinner. She seems in good spirits. Had to unplug the computer to get it to 'shut down' and reboot. Additional complaints about the color of the phone. She wants black. Mom and I are going to begin watching 'Touched By An Angel' on occasion. Good show, even though they're stretching the ubiquitous Angel bit . . . haven't met one myself. Mom would probably like it, at least until that *death* guy makes an appearance.

February 20th, 2004
Gib and Marilyn visited at 3:50 pm. Marilyn called the phone to hear the ring and approved. The ring demands response.

Mom is in good spirits and has applied lipstick. Must be some guy downstairs she wants to impress. Marilyn suggested Jo (when you read this) stop paying the utility bills on the Fairbanks house. If Jason is the present occupant of the house he is the one responsible for the utilities.

Cappy continues to ask if her sons and grandchildren living in Yakima *know where she is*. She asks if Jason is living in her house on Fairbanks.

We tell her 'yes, as far as we know' Jason is still living in the Fairbanks house.

Jason, son, grandson, nephew, former high school athlete, and movie star looks. On the surface every reason for his family to be proud! Physical presence and boyish charm!

And now, years later, he has a wife, (sources say she has a trust fund income) a son, Brendan, and adult responsibilities. He is now addressing those adult responsibilities by living gratuitously in the home of his elderly grandmother who, after paying for Fannie's operation, is now penniless. Her Social Security check barely pays for rent at Evergreen Lodge. Jason has promised again and again to pay the rent he owes...Jo, Gib and Marilyn continue to cover expenses. They are minimal but they add up. We tell her she is not 'broke'! We lie . . .

February 21st, 2004
I arrived and found Cappy visiting with Judy and Fannie. All is looking well with Fannie's eye.

Mom reminisced about the difficulty of getting Al, her last husband, to start any projects needing to be done around the Fairbanks Avenue house in the years they lived there together. Al would complete a project if someone else started it, but the prospect of completing any project from beginning to end, was too overwhelming. Cappy made us laugh when she related the *bed lowering* incident.

She'd decided their bed in the master bedroom was six inches too high off the floor. Could she expect her hard working, hard partying husband to correct this problem for her? No, not without some creative manipulation on her part.

About an hour before Al was supposed to arrive home she took a hacksaw into the bedroom and laboriously sawed off one leg of the bed, lowering one side of one end. Her work created a sloping angle at the head of the bed on the left side and rapidly descended downward to the foot of the bed on the right side. She then went back to the kitchen to finish her cup of coffee.

Al arrived home, ate his dinner and then made for the bedroom for his ritual two hour Friday evening nap, traditional before going on the town to begin his habitual weekend bender. When he saw the bed orchestrated to deliver any body attempting to lie down on it immediately to the floor, he began to swear in German ... Fiesa hock a socka da min!". . . whatever that means.

Cappy, sitting in the kitchen over her cup of coffee, just smiled!

Mom was watching Die Hard when I left fully convinced her mental dexterity could have saved Bruce Willis 'a lotta problems'!

February 22nd, 2004
Arrived to find Cappy watching TV, her focus periodically being interrupted by the eye-catching motion of seagulls gracefully swooping from light standard to pavement, snatching up the tasty morsels dropped by the litter prone customers emerging from the Albertson's store.

I am here to use mom's computer and then I'm off to speak with Harvey and his girlfriend Marie, primarily about the ring and the watch. I typed emails to Jo and Jason. Visited with mom for a few minutes and then left to reunite with Harvey for the first time in thirteen years. Prestigious, haute cuisine? Hardly, we're meeting at a McDonalds.

Harvey, sitting in a booth with a petite Asian woman of indeterminate age, rose and extended his hand. Older, heavier, but still with the great smile and an enviable abundance of dark brown hair, I took his hand and asked, "Where you been?" It was meant as a way to lighten the mood and Harvey seemed to take it that way.

"Here and there," he said. "This is Marie."

I held my hand out to Marie and said, "Hello!" She took my hand. "Hi Gib."

Though I know this woman much better now, I am fully convinced I will never really know her. She is alternately charming and rude, religious and dishonest, caring and distant. Her most dominant trait, then and now, where Harvey is concerned, is jealously. She gives him no measure of commitment but exacts a piece of flesh if he so much as exchanges a greeting with another woman. But all of that would surface later. For now she portrayed herself as nice, sweet, grandmotherly, an Asian Aunt Bea. And my role, that of the ingenuous Opie.

But on this day we discussed many things prior to focusing on the watch and the ring. Among them, where had Harvey been for the last thirteen years? His reason for virtually cutting himself off from his family? He claims I failed to meet him for a luncheon appointment made all those years ago.

I am family oriented and would not have forgotten. A simple phone call could easily have cleared the air.

I heard from Harvey one time in those thirteen years. He asked me to make some phone calls to find out if he was divorced from his second wife, Liz. I did and he was. A simple thank you and back behind the veil for another six or seven years. Same can be said for Harvey's daughter, Renee. Once close to her grandmother, Cappy has not heard from Renee in many years. She asks about Renee, Craig (Mike's son) and of course, Michael Dean (Mike's eldest son, and Lori Jo, his only daughter). Harvey told me the ring and watch were being held by a Russian couple. He has until March 15th to retrieve them.

Renee Edmonson (Harvey's daughter, Cappy's granddaughter)

February 24th, 2004
Marilyn is at the dentist but mom's most frequent, and thus, most boring guest has arrived.

It is midday and once again the Belle of the Ball is on the bed. If she becomes bedridden will they suggest a nursing home? A continued lessening of physical activity seems potentially threatening to her already restricted independence.

She asked what I had been 'up to'?

I said 'looking for nursing homes for you because a nursing home appears to be your next stop.' I explained, hopefully with the correct degree of harshness, emphasizing that her enviable living circumstances at Evergreen Lodge were dependent on maintaining at least a modicum of mobility.

She looked at me. I waited. She said, "Ok, what have you really been up to?"

Incredibly convincing, aren't I?

We haven't heard from Cappy's younger brother Earl in three weeks. Of her six siblings, Earl is the only one remaining. We usually receive two or three emails from him a week. He is in good health but in his mid-eighties. Any extended silence is ominous.

His deceased wife's family, now his family, takes wonderful care of the man they call 'Dad Earl'. My only communication with them has been through email but, given the power, I would canonize them. They are an incredible clan and they take wonderful care of the man I call "The Earl of Lewiston"! I'll check with Diana Lee, Earl's stepdaughter, to see if all is well.

February 25th, 2004
Marilyn and Gib came by about 11:15 to take mom to her doctor's appointment.

Dr. Fang (yes, really) informed us that Cappy has lost seven pounds. Cappy says she is now at her party weight and would like to go dancing but has nothing to wear! What is a woman to do when denied the most basic things to have a good time *out there*?

Forget the dance clubs, mom! How about the activities room of Evergreen Lodge three or four times a week for a start?

Before arriving to visit Cappy, we had been to Mitzel's for a Prime Rib dinner special they'd advertised, one which short-changed Marilyn (thin strips of Prime Rib) and has caused her ongoing angst throughout the evening.

Marilyn, have I told you how much I enjoyed MY prime rib?

Ouch . . .

February 26th, 2004
Gib arrived about 1 pm to visit Cappy. Is Cappy lying down? Or is Cappy laying down?

Damn grammar . . . should have been paying attention all those years from 5th grade through 9th when they attempted to cram grammatical correctness into my brain through the pinhole opening seemingly reserved for advanced knowledge of sports trivia.

Mom, the English genius, is unsure also.

We'll be occupying seats side by side upon our return to elementary school, a combined 150 years of life's experience attempting to learn when to use 'did or done', 'went or gone', 'she or her' and other grammatical pearls that escaped us. I received a columnist offer in my email today; no mention of money so my reply broached the subject.

Cappy's children were taught early; the end result of *work* should be a buck or two!

February 27th, 2004
Gib and Marilyn arrived about 3:30 p.m.

Mom is rebelling! We have asked her to go to extraordinary lengths in an attempt to regain solvency, since no rent is coming this direction from Jason. We explain patiently! In reality, she is a pauper, dependent on the generosity of others and we suggest her reduced circumstances would improve if she were to begin begging on street corners for the dimes and quarters she needs for incidentals like toothpaste.

Her rebellion is taking the form of a refusal to hold the sign that says, "Please help! Will work for toothpaste!" She also states, if forced to hold the sign she will laugh while doing so! We have emphasized the importance of her appearing destitute and if she laughs while holding the sign her chances of making a buck become finite. Her favorite saying as her children emerged from their toddler years was "Make hay while the sun shines!", a phrase now being repeated back to this rebellious woman in her late eighties who is refusing to *hold her sign* and *work* her corner.

Damn, another income opportunity going south on us for lack of ambition . . .

February 28th, 2004

Cappy is in good spirits when her number two son arrives on this day. She wants to talk about her given name, Capitola.

A curly haired, always pleasant staff person named Marnie, has fallen phonetically in love with the name 'Capitola' and, according to Cappy, Marnie seems to experience some sort of melodic joy as she repeats 'Capitola'. It reminds Cappy of the musical *West Side Story* and the young male actor singing the song "Maria".

'Maria! I'll never stop saying' 'Maria Maria, Maria . . . Maria'

Except Marnie hears it as 'Capitola', Capitola, Capitola . . . Capitola. She doesn't want to be rude to the aide but she hates hearing 'Capitola'. I'll solve the problem for her. I'll ask the aide to refrain . . .

How did she come to be named 'Capitola'? Her mother read many books as she awaited the birth of her third daughter. Two of the books were titled, 'The Hidden Hand' and 'Capitola's Peril' and the heroine of both books was a spirited teenager named 'Capitola'.

Roxanne Bowse, Cappy's mother, was a wise and wonderful woman cherished by all of her seven children. Inevitably, as Cappy approached puberty, she began to compare her name with those of her six siblings, Ida, Glen, Lois, Earl, Fred and Vera. When she asked her mother, "Why Capitola?" she received the book heroine answer.

All her life Cappy, in good humor, has maintained that pregnant women shouldn't be allowed to read.

Fannie

March 1st, 2004

It seems a resident named 'Art' complained about Fannie looking a bit 'shaggy'.

In an effort to appease Art, Judy decided to cut Fannie's hair. Another resident, Linda, offered to help. The two of them, with shears limited to just one setting, reduced this abundantly pelted dog to skin and bone. The shears had cut through the skin in several places leaving what appeared to be painful looking cuts.

Both Judy and Linda were apologetic to the extreme.

We've told Judy many times to call us if Fannie needs anything! This incident has put an exclamation point on each of those admonishments. Nothing like it will happen again or we'll make other arrangements for Fannie.

March 2nd, 2004

Cappy's mood is light on this day. She especially enjoys my foibles, my attempts to muddle through each twenty-four hour period without some sort of self-induced calamity.

"What's up?" she asked as I entered the small living room/bedroom of her apartment. Mom doesn't use the word 'cool' as many young people do, but she has adopted the greeting 'What's up?' from somewhere. Eighty-nine years old and each day when I come to see her I'm greeted with, "What's up?" I am way behind her in the correct use of the accepted vernacular of the day.

I am not my ebullient self. Cappy senses it.

"I tore up Marilyn's check stub to prevent her social security number from being stolen."

Cappy merely looks confused. I explain, "She inevitably leaves them lying around and has asked me to tear them up so no one can get her social security number off the stub and steal her identity. I've torn up dozens of her stubs."

"So she asks you to tear them up and you do."

"Yes, but this time her check was attached to it! The stub and the check became multiple tiny squares at the bottom of my wastebasket. She wasn't happy!"

"Oh, oh."

"Uh huh. But I reminded her of my role as protector of her social security number and, once again, I had been successful. This time I was most willing to forgo the usual gold star because I had overachieved by tearing up the stub *and the check.*"

"So she understood," was mom's rejoinder.

Can you call an ill-tempered stare and the threat of physical mayhem upon my person understanding?

"Yeah, pretty much."

We visited for a while and I took my leave, venturing back into a life of ineptitude and danger.

March 3rd, 2004
(Jo's entry.) Got to Cappy's around six. I brought her a couple of Three Musketeer bars and she promptly choked on one of them. I pulled the cord to alert the nurse's office that an emergency was occurring. Minutes went by and mom continued to struggle to breathe. I called 911 and then

remembered someone had told me that raising one arm of a choking person will usually clear a passage and he/she will begin to breathe again. I raised mom's right arm and her breathing immediately became less labored. Mom was scared but breathing easily as a staff person and two firemen simultaneously entered the room.

The firemen said I had done the right thing by raising her arm to clear a passage. They also cautioned me not to squeeze her (Heimlich maneuver) if she is coughing. Coughing indicates air is getting through.

Is pulling the cord tantamount to requesting room service? Or is it meant to announce a possible emergency? Time to ask some questions!

March 4th, 2004
Cappy has chosen to excise all that is not sunshine from her memory. She denies having been married to the intellectual fruit picker, the tree falling logger 'Coug' and Al, the construction worker capable of high decibel epithets in multiple languages. We admonish, 'Cappy, Cappy, five boys and a girl and no husbands? We plead, she smiles.

Nothing good can be achieved by reminding her of bad times so references to the intellectual fruit tramp, the logger and the heavy equipment operator continue to be casual.

Gib (Gary Zimmer son #2)

March 5th, 2004

Informed by the staff person in charge of showers that Cappy is refusing to disrobe and get wet on Saturday mornings when she is scheduled to take her shower. Two weeks now, no shower! So, shower woman escorted me to room 261 where we remonstrated with Cappy over her ongoing challenge to everything hygienic. She said, "I don't want anyone to see me 'nudie'." She said, 'I don't get dirty.' She said, 'My dirt is clean'.

Shower woman stood to one side while I gave mom my velvet version of a 'tongue lashing'. "Mom, you have to take a shower once a week!"

"Who says," she said.

Time to roll out one of the big guns. "Those are the rules," I said.

"I'm an adult. I make my own rules," she said.

The big gun didn't work. I'll try a small one. "Remember when I was a toddler and you began to teach me 'cleanliness was next to Godliness'?" Remember how you taught me to wash my hair by rubbing the soap into my scalp with my fingers? Remember when you taught me to wash my ears out, but carefully?"

"Yes" she said, expectantly, wholly prepared for the words of wisdom sure to come next, words of power and words with impact. Suddenly I thought of the brilliance of Edgar Allen Poe and 'The Raven' and 'nevermore' and uttered "Well," . . . like the pitiable sparrow I am.

Meekly, I agreed to be at Evergreen at 11 a.m. the following day to offer shower woman another opportunity to witness my elevated ability to persuade.

March 6th, 2004
Arrived at Evergreen Lodge bright and early to ensure that mom 'agrees' to take her shower.

Mom says, "I have already taken my shower!"

Uh huh . . . well she does have clean clothes on and her hair is curly in the back where she usually flattens it out when she lies down. Could it be?

Staff shower person is not around so . . . I will wander the halls until I find her. Upon leaving the elevator I see shower woman at the end of the hall. When she sees me she immediately gives me the 'thumbs up' sign.

Shower woman and I dance around each other and then hug never considering that the real heroine of this episode of 'Cappy' is upstairs repeating to herself 'docile is good'!

We cherish all of our victories large and small.

March 7th, 2004
I have come to visit Cappy for a few minutes before trekking to Seattle to meet with Harvey and Marie and, hopefully, accomplish the rescue of the Rolex watch and gold ring from the Russian couple holding them ransom.

Harvey agrees, I will hold the watch and the ring until he repays me the six hundred and sixty dollars tendered for said watch and ring, payment to be made within ninety days. Before leaving, I spend a few minutes with Cappy.

I meet Harvey and Marie at McDonalds. Harvey and I go to the Russian's office where I hand over the six hundred and sixty dollars to a rotund, taciturn man of middle age. Without a word, he goes to a safe and retrieves the watch and the ring and hands them to me. I ask about 'documentation', receipts, proof of exchange of money for jewelry. He gives me a menacing look and states, "I did Harvey a favor. I have the money. You have the watch and the ring. Leave!"

Well, ok . . .

Watch and ring in hand, Harvey convinces me he needs the watch. The milk of human kindness and brotherly love pouring from every orifice, I give him the watch. Big mistake . . .

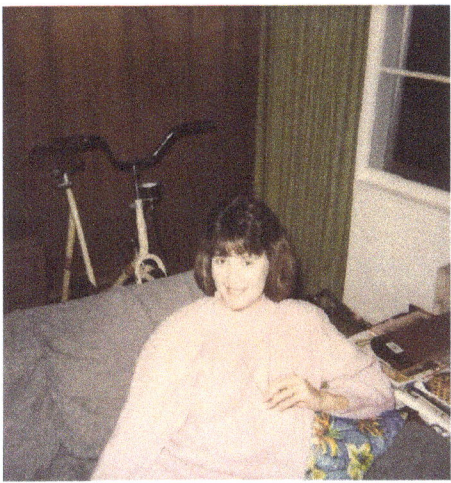

Marilyn Zimmer (Cappy's daughter-in-law)

March 8th, 2004
Mom is asking me questions that, if answered truthfully, will incriminate me. What inspires these questions from this eighty-nine year old woman who believes she raised nothing but perfect children?

Cheech and Chong movies!

She loves them! Never one to drink and having given up Lucky Strikes (LSMFT, Lucky Strikes Mean Fine Tobacco, and they are mild!) thirty-five years ago, I find it amusing that my mother is now a fan of movies owing their success to the joy derived from and the pandemonium created by, the consumption of an illegal substance.

So, she asks, "Have you ever smoked that stuff?"

And I answer, "Several times in the seventies when I was much too weak to say 'no' to attractive women who thought it would be fun to 'get high'."

"What about Marilyn?" Easier to answer this one. "Well, mom, Marilyn was a victim of circumstance or the beneficiary of circumstance, whichever one you choose."

"Tell me!" she asks.

"Everyone cringes at the words 'root canal' and Marilyn is worse than most when forced to confront a dentist and needles. So, you can imagine my surprise when she emerged from the ordeal of her only root canal with a huge smile on her face and an unusual 'energetic' bounce to her step."

"What did they give her?' mom asked, mouth open wide, incredulous.

"Sodium Pentothal, better known as laughing gas, earphones with piped in music and a totally new attitude toward the dental experience."

March 9th, 2004
Arrived with a trap set for Cappy on this sunny March day.

I am armed with her son Harvey's Birth Certificate. On this certificate is the real given name of her second husband, Harvey's father, Johnny 'Coug' Edmonson.

Well, it's John, right?

No, this man of the forest nicknamed for a ferocious feline was burdened with the given first name of 'Heltzle'.

With a mischievous glint in my eye, fully certain she has forgotten her second husband's given first name, and feeling superior for having learned something of her past that has likely escaped her memory, I ask, "What was Johnny Edmonson's 'real' first name?"

"Heltzle," she delivers without hesitation.

Hmmm . . . the wily veteran has escaped again.

Almost seven decades have gone by! I am wrung dry of the minute sense of superiority I entered the room with.

"Heltzle," she says, once again for emphasis, as if the first arrow had not done its work.

"How can you remember that after seventy years?" I ask.

My mother, bless her heart, looks at me as if confronting a crazy man and says, "For God sakes, Gib, I was married to the man!"

I concede her victory and restrain myself from asking her what she had for lunch.

March 10th, 2004
Cappy's most frequent visitors? Me, the ubiquitous Gib, her daughter, the semi-ubiquitous Jo, and, on this day, the femme fatale, the translucent but dazzling Marilyn, who is most willing to accommodate us with a smile and a bit of conversation and then, exhausted, falls asleep. I notice the almost ninety-year old Cappy is also snoozing.

I slip out and descend to chat with a couple of the residents in the activities room.

March 11th, 2004
I called mom about 11:30 and asked her not to eat lunch because Marilyn and I will take her to IHOP. She agreed but, where was she when we came to pick her up . . . at lunch.

The two women she eats with seem somewhat protective of her, urging her to eat and laughing when she says, 'I don't want to get fat!' So, she has developed a rapport with them . . . if only she would build on it and allow some of *the other* residents to enjoy her sense of humor!

Her tablemates say Cappy does appear for most meals but, doesn't eat much! They're working on her to eat more and 'steal fewer coffee cups'. She has six or seven of them in her room.

We went to lunch and mom had chicken strips and fries. When we approached IHOP she said . . . I hop, you hop, everyone hops . . . I asked her if she had been to IHOP before and she said, 'Only with you and Marilyn a couple of weeks ago . . . right on top of it! Brought her home and she, once again is happily ensconced in her chair.

March 12th, 2004
Marilyn and Gib visited Cappy. We're watching a grown up Lee Ann Rimes being interviewed by Jane Pauley. Lee Ann has grown up . . . way up!

Mom says she is happy that we come to visit . . . since it gets 'lonely'.

Having repeatedly challenged her to join the swarms of people downstairs and the multitude of activities taking place in the building, I now tell her Marilyn, myself, Jo, Harvey and Marie are the only people left on earth.

"What about the people downstairs?" she asks. "They're just robots," I answer.

"Oh", she says . . . while secretly wondering when I became crazy . . .

March 13th, 2004
Arrived here with Marilyn about 3:30 p.m. Cappy on the bed . . . but levitating, halfway to heaven, the Almighty must be undecided . . . or called away while in the process of transitioning Cappy. We were able to get her back to the bed and then into her chair so the 'Transitioner' would be confused when he returned to complete his task.

Divine intervention from a different direction . . . awaiting potential repercussions for 'messing' with the SOP of the transitional process . . .

Cappy has a cold . . . sneezing and runny nose. Many Evergreen Lodge residents are beset with the same malady, a staff person tells us.

March 14th, 2004
Harvey arrived at Evergreen Lodge accompanied by his girlfriend, Marie. First time in six years Harvey has seen his mother. Mom was in seventh heaven seeing the long lost son who lived so close but didn't appear, apparently because of his obligations to the CIA (tongue in cheek, everyone).

So, Cappy now has three of her children visiting on a frequent basis. Plus one daughter-in-law, and, lest we forget, Harvey's significant other, Marie . . . who is also a welcome addition to Cappy's visitors list. Cappy is doing well on this day . . . ensconced on her bed watching 'Crocodile Hunter'. We notice Marie has left a small Bible for mom to read . . . will she? We all have our concept of heaven and my lonely voice believes all those with good hearts get a free pass . . .

Mom states emphatically that she would not want to be 'a crocodile hunter' for fear she might find one. Wisdom . . .

March 15th, 2004
Harvey and Marie with mom on this day. Marie's daughter landed a job with Boeing . . . good news! She's been looking for roughly five months. It seems Marie is an accomplished pianist! She played for some of the residents downstairs, receiving accolades and applause. In addition, this fine woman plays the piano for another group of elderly folks in an assisted living center in Seattle . . . each Sunday . . . sans Harvey . . . to his chagrin. "I want my Marie", seems to be his Sunday mantra . . . nothing wrong with that . . . he is attached, awash in fondness . . . love prevailing over all . . .

March 16th, 2004
Gib visited . . . found mom standing in total darkness except for a sliver of light entering the room from the Albertson's parking lot. She greeted me but didn't move from the place she was standing. I asked her why she was standing in the dark and she

replied, "I started to do something and now I can't remember what it was."

I understood perfectly, happens to me all the time. I suggested a couple of things she might have had in mind when she left her sitting position on the bed. Neither jogged her memory.

I asked why the lights weren't on and, in keeping with the mystery of the moment, she said she didn't know. Using the minimal light provided by the light standards from the parking lot next door, I walked over to the switch and flipped it. Nothing. No lights and the TV was off so I assumed there wasn't any power.

We waited, and then I recalled, the lights in the hall were on. I walked over to her cupboard, opened it and extracted a light bulb. I placed a chair beneath the ceiling light, stood on the chair and reached above the ornamental glass fixture shielding the bulb from view, unscrewed the bulb, replaced it with the new one and . . . light!

Sometimes, the simplicity of her world becomes an invitation easily accepted.

Harvey walked in as we were talking about him. Mom knew he was coming before he 'appeared.' I asked her how she knew and she said 'I saw his reflection in the window.' So much for her magical powers.

March 17th, 2004
Doctors visit for Cappy tomorrow at 1:20. Marilyn and I will escort her. Cappy knows all is well . . . says she's only going to give the Doctor peace of mind.

Jo
It's spring training and the Mariners are getting ready for another season of futility! Mom loves the games win or lose. She would watch baseball all day long if she could.

March 18th, 2004
Marilyn and Gib arrived at 4:05! Cappy is sitting in her chair watching TV. She says she doesn't go down to dinner and when

she does, 'no one knows who she is.' Many people in the building know her by her first name . . . but she forgets.

She tells us she can see the bottom of Mt. Rainier but that clouds obscure the mountain's top. What a view! She wants to know why nature chose to put a mountain there. Gib told her the answer to that question is 'for you'!

Cappy is happy with her mountain . . .

Cappy's accumulation of coffee cups is creating an abundance of them in her room and a shortage of them in the dining room. Before I left I gathered five or six cups which I then delivered to Luuk in the office. He just gave me a knowing smile and thanked me.

March 19th, 2004
A sunny March day! Gib visited. Cappy smiled as he entered and asked 'What's up' while she continued watching the erudite Dr. Phil. Gib, noting how tidy and orderly Cappy's apartment is and recalling the state of disorder and clutter upon his desk before he left home, declared he needed help getting organized.

The always neat and orderly Cappy suggested he go on Dr. Phil and get some counseling for his organizational woes?

Gib suggested Cappy would make a better subject to be interviewed knowing Dr. Phil would be captivated by this octogenarian's homespun wisdom and humor. He could counsel her on her inability to choose a life partner who would bring her the joy she so deserved, and Cappy, quickly passing by his advice because she had discovered peace and tranquility could be attained without a *man*, then would advise Dr. Phil that his ability to heal the mind could be augmented with the magical powers of 'wirecut' and its ability to heal the body, thereby fully earning the title of Doctor. She would, of course, suggest a different name for Earl Bowse Senior's wonderful potion.

March 20th, 2004

Gib visited and set up mom's VCR. Now we can watch movies with her. Friday evenings might work.

Mom hates the color of her phone. She wants traditional black and one allowing her to step back into the seventies when all of us had the pleasure of dialing 7 numbers to reach out to someone. I suggested she and Jo should talk about it and come up with a plan.

After twenty-six years of running a business requiring that I spend 3 or 4 hours of each day on the phone . . . would like to forget they exist . . . except of course when I actually need one.

March 21st, 2004
Jo

I've stopped by several times but haven't written in the journal . . . the phone color . . . oh well, let's wait a while and mom will more than likely take to the color . . . if not . . . ???

Amanda

Mom is concerned that Tony and Rick may not know where she is and seeing them will give her peace of mind but, she has asked about Amanda several times. Hopefully, we can make arrangements for her to see Amanda too.

(Amanda and Gordie, daughter and son of Sharon, Tony's significant other for several years, were often dropped off at Cappy's for babysitting and she came to consider them as equal to her own grandchildren. When Amanda grew up and became a meat cutter at Safeway, Cappy often called upon Amanda to help her with grocery shopping. Amanda, gracious and giving, always obliged Cappy when called upon.)

March 22nd, 2004
Jo

The Jason situation is disappointing to say the least. I was hoping he'd sent you some money. Let's sell it!. Hope you are doing well, we'll talk soon.

March 23rd, 2004

'My back hurts' Cappy declares as her second son enters on this day, his birthday. Back pain? Could this be some atavistic revisiting of pain from a long ago day in 1939 when she brought me into this world? Unlikely, so I address the back issue.

"When did that start?"

"Just the last couple of days," she replies.

"If it persists we'll have it checked out."

"Happy Birthday!" she says smiling.

"Thank you. You remembered."

"Of course I remembered!"

"Are you still sixteen?" I asked.

"Yup, still sixteen.'

Cappy (forever sixteen)

"I'm your son and I'm older than you are. How can that be?"

"Things were less complicated when I was sixteen. I just decided it was a good age to be. I had two more good years after that before stuff started to happen."

Meaning she married the intellectual fruit tramp at nineteen.

However, during the harsh years of the Depression, in a family of six siblings, Cappy was the only one of the seven to graduate from high school. In addition to her schoolwork she contributed to the family fortunes by taking in ironing and helping her mother clean the homes of a few of those 'up on the hill' folks, as Roxanne Bowse called the well-to-do families of Lewiston.

The sixteen year old helped me find the elevator and then skipped back down the hall to room 261.

March 24th, 2004
Gib & Jo arrived here about an hour apart. Discussed Jason saying he was going to try to make it over on Sunday (the 28th). Hope it happens . . . mom would love to see him.

March 25th, 2004
One of the staff encouraged mom to go downstairs and watch bingo. She did and that is where she was (activity room) when Marilyn and I arrived. Judy was playing bingo (w/fannie by her side). We visited in the hallway until almost time for mom's dinner. Gradually, Cappy is becoming more social and confident with her surroundings. Walked her to the dining room and left in search of food to sustain us for another day . . .

March 26th, 2004
My visit on this Friday coincided with Jo's. While Cappy watched TV Jo and I discussed the circumstances of Cappy's expenses in the hallway.

Jo
I'm not paying on the house bills. If things get turned off then it's up to Jason! He hasn't come through with any money in any form! I think it's time we forced the issue. I'll call him tomorrow and find out what his plan is.

Gib
Eventually, the house will be sold and the money derived from the sale can be used to pay her expenses. Our attempts to help Jason and his family required that he pay the minimal rent and

the utilities on the Fairbanks house. Unfortunately, he has failed to keep his part of the bargain . . . all bets are off at this point. We'll begin preparing the house for sale.

March 27th, 2004
Gib & Marilyn brought a large bowl of MZ's famous beef soup for mom. Judy and Fannie are here visiting and it appears Fannie is gaining weight while Cappy is losing, and neither has any awareness or concern regarding these miniscule changes within the universe. Cappy declares, I get plenty of exercise walking around in my room!" Plus the several trips she makes each day up and down the corridors just outside her door . . .

Uh huh . . . and the moon really is made of blue cheese . . .

March 28th, 2004
Gib and Marilyn visited. Jo was here and all of us talked about Mom's financial situation. Jo gave us $80 for Fannie's grooming and mom's phone bill. Receipts for phone bill on desk.

Change of plans. Jason is now planning to visit on Wednesday the 31st.

March 29th, 2004
Well, I've been questioning the worth of this journal thing, since I am the only one who writes in it and reads from it . . . and this isn't exactly as historically significant as the words of Samuel Pepys . . .

March 30th, 2004
Gib brought mom a Hershey bar and a drink to take Barley Green with. We'll try this stuff and see if there's any noticeable difference in energy, vitality and memory. I checked mom's account . . . no deposits. I'll call Rick later today and see if he has a 'plan'. Mom hasn't complained about her back in a while. Not being in the bed so much, I believe, helps with the back situation.

She says this *clicking* (my typing) makes her sleepy . . . and wants me to come over when it's time for her to take a nap . . . nice to be good for something!

March 31st, 2004
Jo
Jason is supposed to be here later today, but I'm not mentioning it to mom so as not to get her hopes up.

April 1st, 2004
Jo and Harvey visited on this April Fool's Day. Cappy teased Harvey about his boyish good looks at sixty-three. It's the hair . . . Harvey dyes it . . .

April 2nd, 2004
Gib visiting. Before even greeting me, Cappy asked, 'Can they say that on television?' Before I could answer I heard a reference to *panther urine* from one of the characters on the screen. As I began to reply to her question Cappy changed the channel saying 'Not my kind of show' . . . and I knew without asking, her earlier question of 'can they say that on television' made reference to something more offensive to her than *panther urine* and it led me to consider why one person finds humor and embraces an edgy line and another, like Cappy, has heard the worst the world has to offer verbally, but would prefer her humor to be absent of profanity? But, *to each their own, live and let live, one man's meat is another man's poison* . . . and all of that . . . but, like Cappy, I'm passing on any more episodes of 'Whoopi' . . .

Brought some Barley Green in Slimfast and mom liked the taste. We tried to call Jo to wish her a happy birthday (mom believes this is her daughter's birthday) . . . is it? We aren't sure. Mom tells me her memory is 'shot' . . . yes, but there is still a twinkle in her eye, she is moving well and she laughs often . . . of those things we can control . . . what else matters?

Jason was a no show.

Cappy and grandchildren Kari and Mark (Gib's daughter and son)

April 3rd, 2004

Kari called me last evening and asked about 'Nana'. Said she would make it here for lunch in the next week or so. I'm going to leave about 3:30.

No, we haven't heard from Jason. I would guess he's moved out of the house by now. Marilyn and I (with mom) are planning a trip over in two weeks. If Jo is available we would like her to go with us.

Jo

Mom does seem to be doing well. I came to see her last week and found her in the hall (downstairs) visiting with several people. Most encouraging!

Regarding the trip across the mountain, I'm only available on April 24th. I know your plan is for mom to see Tony and Rick but another objective should be to assess the condition of the Fairbanks house and decide what needs to be done to get it ready for sale. We'll make a list . . . I'm good at lists!

Earl Bowse Jr.

April 4th, 2004

Cappy, octogenarian, soon to be centenarian, frequently expresses her appreciation of 'high tech'. "I'm sure glad the computer is here!" she states. Hope immediately springs to the surface of my being . . . as I recall the late nineties when I spent many evenings with mom at her kitchen table in Yakima trying to impart the basics of a Compaq desktop to her. Her memory was better then and she retained some of the information and, ultimately, used what she learned to send emails to her brother Earl in Lewiston, Idaho. She, as I did, when first exposed to the computer as a tool, described it as *magical,* somewhat unbelieving of the computer's ability to help the common man with so many tedious and cumbersome tasks. But, on this day, she was not appreciating the computer as a tool; instead she credited it for 'bringing people here' and providing company for her. I immediately corrected her.

"Mom, I don't come here because of the computer. I come here to see you! Jo comes here to see you!" I emphasize, "If the computer is here and you aren't . . . I'm not coming here!"

"Am I going somewhere?" Well, not yet . . . we hope!

April 5th, 2004
Came to see mom about 4 pm and we have a mystery brewing. She has received two calls today for Marie, Harvey's significant other. I answered the second call and spoke with Mike from Discover Financial Services. Why is Cappy's telephone number being used for Marie to solicit a loan? Is her address also being used as Marie's address? I'll ask some questions of Harvey and Marie and resolve this hint of identity theft before 'Capitola' of the Hidden Hand is called upon to *return* and save her elderly namesake.

Yes, I will implement determination and resourcefulness . . . there is a bit of the *Perry Mason* and *Columbo* in me...and MZ in the background mutters quietly . . . more like Della Street . . .

Marie and Harvey are good to mom and visit a lot . . . so if using this number is helpful to them and not injurious to her in any way, I have no complaint. As long as it doesn't become too much of a problem for mom getting up and down to answer the phone . . . hmmmm . . . exercise . . .

April 6th, 2004
Gib visited Cappy on this fine day. Mom is a bit 'raspy' and possibly getting a cold.

Fortuitously (but not with Marie in mind), we watched a program on identity theft. Cappy, insightful as ever, concluded that anyone watching this show who may be in need of a buck or two, now has a perfect blueprint to resolve their problem.

I should have recorded it. Cappy's children may have need of that buck or two as the Cappy saga plays out.

April 7th, 2004
Jo
I'm back from the brink of death by cold. Helped mom take a bath . . . she rinsed me off instead of herself so I'm taking my soaking wet jeans and going home now.

April 10th, 2004

I'm visiting with Cappy and we just solved all Divine issues. Mom and I decided God loves us and will forgive the few mistakes we make along the way, not throw us into a fiery pit for eternity. This came up because mom remembered her father had said, 'as a *mortal man* I could not throw one of my children into a fire, so how could God do it in the name of love and forgiveness.' Whew, glad she agrees with me on that one!

April 11th, 2004

Cappy is one year shy of being a centenarian. When the subject is brought up she doesn't want to talk about it, but agrees, still being able to talk about it, if she chooses to . . . is a good thing!

Cappy is doing well! She is decked out in her pajamas and watching TV. She is impressed with Fannie's new look. Fannie is right at home with her, remembering the many years they spent together in the Fairbanks house. Having Judy care for Fannie and periodic visits with Cappy has worked out well. Jo is at a seminar in some southern state.

All is well in Cappyland except for her insistence on wearing the new red shirt Marilyn purchased for her (3 others as well) every day, saying she loves the feel of it and, she emphasizes, 'it's RED'. Ok, but you have to change *once in a while*.

Jen Saunderson (Lori's daughter, Mike's granddaughter)

April 12th, 2004
Cappy continues to ask about Lori Jo, her deceased son Michael's daughter. We believe Lori lives in Bellingham just north of Seattle and on this day I informed Cappy that an ad was placed in the Bellingham Herald reading, "Lori Jo, daughter of Rosalie and Mike, sister of Michael Dean, please contact Gary Zimmer 253-927-4207".

Hope she sees it.

Harvey asked for his ring back. Said he 'just wants to wear it, not hock it." The ring was being held as security for a $660 loan we advanced Harvey to secure the ring and his watch from a Russian jeweler holding it for him as a favor.

I informed Harvey that I would not be a source of financial help in the future. He agreed and took the ring.

April 13th, 2004
Gib visited. Cappy is in good spirits, Hershey bar wrappers everywhere. I believe Harvey and Marie gave her some help with the bars.

April 14th, 2004
Gib is visiting. Cappy and I laughed over the Reindeer joke Diana Lee sent. I brought her a new comb replacing the one I inadvertently purloined about 3 weeks ago.

She sounds raspy. I have to start getting here early enough to walk the halls with her. She isn't getting enough exercise. It is

4:24 and time for mom to go down to dinner. Three Hershey bar survivors are sitting within reach of her and a couple of chocolate cookies are on her night stand. We sent off an email to Uncle Earl after receiving a short note from him.

Cappy continually emphasizes, 'I'm glad I quit smoking all those years ago!' I reminded her of the *free cigarettes* (nicotine free) Jo brought home years ago, allowing her to quit so easily. She laughed remembering how incredibly messy the ashes from those cigarettes were. They would persevere into a long curling cylinder, the cylinder refused to drop from the cigarette into an ashtray, but would immediately fall to the table once moved away from above the ashtray. Decades of use, a month or so to quit . . . and maybe she quit just in time to allow her about twenty plus years of peace of mind.

April 15th, 2004
I am at Evergreen Lodge visiting Cappy. I'm looking down at the Albertson's Supermarket parking lot and realizing I forgot the movies I rented from Albertson's the other day and now I can't exchange them! So much for organization . . .

Cappy is watching TV . . . Marilyn is where? . . . shopping!

Harvey is here and wondering where the three gold chains Marie gave Cappy have gone to. Now that we are suspicious of Marie's character, the distinct possibility exists that Marie may have needed a few bucks and changed her mind about giving Cappy the chains. And then again, there may be other reasons the chains have disappeared.

Time for Cappy to go down to dinner.

April 16th, 2004
Forgot them (movies) again too! Cappy says 'aging is a curse' . . . but, she says it with a smile.

Cappy declares, "I miss driving!" Cappy learned to drive in her mid-fifties and became a good driver. She loved the ability to get into her car and run her errands instead of having to depend on others for rides. Also, I believe she was preparing for the future when the construction guy would no longer be a part of her life and a time when she would need mobility to exist.

Years went by taking a toll on her reactions and awareness. Ultimately, the time came for Cappy to give up driving. But, as with many seniors, she did not agree.

One of her son Rick's objectives when he was visiting his mother was to ensure the battery cables to her car were disconnected. Cappy always asked any male visitor to check her car to see why it wouldn't start. Meaning well, they would reconnect the battery cables giving her the peace of mind knowing the car would be operable in the event of an emergency. To save his mother grief and possible injury, not to speak of the potential of injury to others, on his next visit, Rick would again disconnect the cables. Knowing Cappy was not on the road probably gave him a sense of security regarding his own safety, and others; good choice!

April 17th, 2004
Cappy says the reason she doesn't join in the activities here at Evergreen is *she is too lazy*. I warned that creeping laziness could lead to total lack of movement and *total lack of movement* could be misunderstood. She could be hauled away, completely too lazy to let them know she has been *overcome* with laziness but, is still breathing!

"Put me down! Put me down!"

April 18th, 2004
Gib is visiting. It suddenly occurred to me today that my son Mark is thirty-seven. How can it be? How can it have been thirty-seven years since I was under the house on Richey Road with a blow torch trying to unfreeze the pipes because we had a new baby in the house? Can't be! Thank God the years are not going by as fast for me as they are for Mark! Well, you get to be my age 'ya gotta lie a little'.

Cappy is doing well after a weekend of much activity. Her grandson, Michael Dean (Lori Jo's brother), the man of many tattoos, came all the way from San Diego to see her. He is a rough looking sort, an ex-con, who has developed an easy approach to life, laughs easily and encourages others to do the same, doesn't drink though he lives between two bars, and gave up smoking so he could 'continue to breathe' as he put it. Success is being at peace with yourself and the life you're living. His physical appearance doesn't reflect it . . . but, my guess is . . . Michael Dean is successful.

Michael Dean has no pictures of his father. We searched and found 12 photos of Mike at different ages in mom's albums. Jo had them duplicated and now, Michael Dean, who worshiped his wayward father, has a pictorial record of the strong, but weak, Michael Roy Zimmer. Michael Dean left for San Diego Sunday, promising to sign off on mom's house whenever the paperwork reached him.

April 19th, 2004
I sent author J.A. Jance a copy of 'Yes, You're Still My Mother.' She said it caused her to get a bit *weepy* since her mother is ninety and experiencing some of what mom is going through. There is a plus side to aging. I think mom is really enjoying herself these days. Her words, the other day, smiling big, "I just enjoy life."

April 20th, 2004
Marilyn and I are here to get Cappy down to the hair salon. She is resisting . . . says she doesn't need to have her hair washed. We emphasized, it should be done once a week . . . at least. Cappy says, 'It should be up to the person.' Sanitation . . . Cappy says, 'my scalp isn't oily. I'm not scratching my head like some people do.' How often should a person have their hair washed? Cappy says, 'That should be up to them!'

Then she told us an amusing story. Cappy said, 'All of life's necessities were precious growing up in South Dakota, water and food more than anything else. When it rained it came down in buckets. Living just outside of Sioux Falls, mom used to have us kids take what she called 'hill folks' baths. At the first sign of storm clouds she would send the boys to the front yard and the girls to the back, each holding a bar of soap. All would strip to their bare skin and wait.

When the heavy South Dakota rains came down, each of her children would spread soap from head to foot and vigorous rubbing would begin. After a thorough scrubbing each child would be thrown a towel to dry with. Then all would get dressed and come back into the house smiling as clean as a rain washed rock.'

What about those harsh South Dakota winters, mom?

"Don't remember", she said.

April 21st, 2004
Gib visiting Cappy. I believe providing mom with an energy/vitamin drink (Ensure?) is a good idea in view of her preference for Hershey bars over actual food.

My morning meal was a Slim Fast shake. When I told Cappy this she said, 'You're not eating very well, either.' I told her I was trying to lose about five pounds. She looked at me like I was crazy. 'You don't need to lose any weight.' I told her, 'when I'm stripped down I see a bulge here and there'. She says, 'well I don't have to see you that way'. She thought a moment and said, 'neither do you if you avoid mirrors'.

A mother's wisdom!

April 22nd, 2004
I am visiting Cappy but only for a few minutes. Not able to stay long, I want my presence to have impact. I say one word and immediately capture Cappy's attention.

"Wirecut", I say.

"Wirecut", she responds, "what do you know about 'wirecut'?

I reply, "I know *wirecut* was your father's home remedy and it could cure anything from acne to gaping wounds of the flesh."

A twinkle in her eye, she says, "My father, your grandfather! What a piece of work he was!", again demonstrating her agile ability to wield present day vernacular. "And that wirecut was miraculous stuff."

I had spent a portion of my ninth year in Lewiston, Idaho, living with my grandmother, grandfather and my uncle, Earl Jr. At this stage of his life, Earl Sr.'s physical miseries precluded any attempt to bond with my rambunctious ways, other than to administer his magical formula after I had gotten the worst of whomever or whatever I had collided with.

He would admonish me to be 'more careful' next time. He would say, "This will hurt a little bit", and then he would apply the *wirecut*. The sting would make me say, "Ouch, ouch, ouch," but in no time the wound would heal over and I would be ready for my next losing battle.

I remember only one time when Earl Sr.'s iron masked facade slipped. I had written a letter to my mother who, with Harvey, was living with my great Aunt Edith in Hermiston, Oregon, while she gathered a financial foundation between marriages. In the letter, I pleaded with her to attend a function at the grade school I was attending, the same grade school she had attended as a child.

She wrote back that she couldn't be there.

We were at the kitchen table when I read my mother's response to my request. My eyes moistened and my nine-year old composure began to slide. The daunting presence of my grandfather, a man who dealt with physical pain every waking hour, a man who had never said a kind word to me, put his hand lightly on my shoulder and said without a hint of hostility toward his daughter, "Gib, I'm going to kick her butt next time I see her."

I looked up and he was smiling at me. Another new occurrence! I smiled back and all was well. That was as close as we ever came to being grandfather and grandson in the conventional sense. But we had an agreement regarding the radio at six thirty and 7 p.m. At six thirty he could listen to

Gabriel Heater. Then at seven he had to endure 'The Adventures of the Lone Ranger' with me.

Maybe if I had spent time with him when I was younger, say six, we might have been better friends. Instead of my grandfather or my father, I got Heltzle!

Cappy, what were you thinking?

Back to the present. "Wirecut!", mom says, once again. "Dad's solution to everything, bleeding or not. He was a good man, not perfect, but a good man. The smartest thing he ever did was marry your grandmother."

No doubt!

'Wirecut' revisited, our salute to Earl Bowse Sr. ended.

April 23rd, 2004
Fannie, Gib and Marilyn came to visit with the resident of room 261. Fannie came with us . . . unleashed . . . she is a good dog who continues to look over her shoulder to make sure we're following. Fannie is looking good since growing some hair back and walks with the same dignity and pride common to her before she was so shamefully shorn . . .

April 24th, 2004
We are here to escort Cappy to the doctor's office for the purpose of having her thyroid checked. If not eager to go there, she is at least willing. Looking good in a blue blouse, the gray one of the last four days finally discarded in favor of a clean and festive looking blue one. We are off to see the Wizard of thyroids.

After thyroid blood drawing we gave Cappy her choice, back to her room or having lunch somewhere. Decided on lunch at Country Buffet. Cappy ate well, topping everything off with chocolate cake and Vanilla ice cream.

We will now conduct a search for her sunglasses. Misplaced! Yup, misplaced in her sunglasses case and in plain sight right beside the computer. No need to call Columbo . . .

April 25th, 2004
Marilyn and Gib visited Cappy. She seems in good spirits while watching TV and eating her lunch. Cappy declares, "I don't have much interest in going down for meals." But, we have stressed to her the importance of exercise and acknowledging that she is not Royalty, and not being Royalty, she needs to make it as easy as possible for Staff to keep her happy. They have been really good about bringing meals to her. Time for her to become more active again . . . she agrees.

April 26th, 2004
Errands, personal missions, no visit to mom today! Maybe Jo, Harvey and Marie . . . no doubt someone was there to visit...no journal entry though . . .darn!

April 27th, 2004
Gib visited and discussed the book, Liberty Falling, which having read, Gib disliked. First serving for me from Nevada Barr (contribution from Jo) and couldn't figure out why I didn't like it. Mom picked up the book and immediately started laughing. Didn't stop for 20 minutes. Everything she read was funny. She read me passages and, damned if they weren't funny! So much for my ability to appreciate good writing.

Marilyn is at the Fair with her son. Better them than me! No sign of Harvey which is a bit unusual for Friday and Saturday. Dart season begins today. I am prepared to be torn and tattered at the end of the day . . . fitting result for someone who can't appreciate a good book!

April 28th, 2004
Marilyn and Gib visited. Judy and Fannie came up for a few minutes. Between Marilyn and Jo, mom's room is looking pretty good. The bed was approaching the status of a bed without room for that important 'sleeping person' who justifies its unique designation.

April 29th, 2004
Cappy and I are reminiscing about the early childhood of her offspring, stating she must have done a good job because 'no

one went to jail'. Pollyanna has descended and taken over mom's body.

May 1st, 2004
Cappy is well. She is wearing her warm up jacket and ready for her daily jog . . . oh yeah . . . She has chocolate chip cookies and a Nestle crunch bar next to the bed, reading Agatha Christie and listening to Eminem blasting forth on the Telly! Life is good when you're an octogenarian.

She is wearing the same blouse we had her change into last week. How can we get her to change each day? There are several reasons, hygiene of course, but also as a flight from tedium?

Almost time for her dinner. Will visit again tomorrow and bring an episode of 'Becker' which she has grown fond of . . .

May 2nd, 2004
Gib visited. Mom in good spirits with chocolate chip cookies winking at her from beside the ever present (occupied 23 hours a day) bed. She is on day three with the same blouse. She has nothing else to wear *she states sadly,* refusing to acknowledge the 7 or 8 new blouses in her closet. After one more day of continuous wear and this blouse too will be pilfered by some rotten no good thief.

Mom is concerned about the thief. Doesn't want to lose another of her favorite pieces of clothing. She is more than willing to change into something new to save her old standby blouse. She is, once again, displaying the superior common sense that has allowed her to survive these many years.

May 3rd, 2004
I called Cappy the other day and just before we hung up I asked her to go out in the hall and walk for the exercise. She said, "I will but not right now . . . I'm busy." I asked her what she was busy doing and she said, justifiably, "I don't think that's any of your business!" Ok, sorry I asked . . . hung up the phone and laughed for five minutes.

May 4th, 2004
Gib arrived to see Cappy of room 261. Found mom, once again on the bed, in good spirits and prepared to welcome visitors, if she had any. Shortly after my arrival, Judy appeared with Fannie. All of us had a good visit. Fannie is doing well, a bit fat but happy to see her friend of many years. Seems she *nipped* another one of the staff members.

Repercussions could follow . . .

May 5th, 2004
Gib visited . . . Harvey sitting here with mom, sulking. He isn't happy when Marie does her Sunday thing without him.

The check issued by Jo (through mom) for Harvey's August rent is not cashable because the amount was changed from $600 to $645. Even though the change was initialed, his bank would not cash the check. I'll handle it by taking it to my bank, Harvey in tow, tomorrow.

May 6th, 2004
Gib arrived to deal with the check. Harvey and I went to Bank of America and were told they could not cash the check because the payee did not have an account with their bank . . . well, as it turns out Harvey does have an account with them . . . but is overdrawn by $28. Gib consults his wallet and forks over the $28, BofA accepts the check but will not release the funds until they have been guaranteed five days later. Not a problem . . . the money will be in Harvey's account on the ninth . . . rent handled . . . through mom, Jo, Gib, Bank of America, Capital One . . . and finally, Harvey. September looms but so does Harvey's unemployment benefits . . . whoop te doo . . .

May 7th, 2004
Jo
Arrived here around 6. Brought mom a couple of 3 Musketeer bars. She's happy. I turned the fan on since she said she didn't know how. Also, on this really warm day, the heat was on!

(Mom is getting a hint of what awaits her if she encounters problems on *the other side...)*

I turned on the Mariners and I'm heading home.

May 8th, 2004

Gib visited. Mom sitting in her chair, no TV going. A concerted effort to locate the remote control resulted in success. It was hiding in the bedcovers. Turned on the TV and immediately discovered the quiet of the room was preferable to the hypnotic monotony of daytime television. Breaking the silence Cappy says she is giving up Hershey bars and going back to smoking, stating she was 'getting too fat'. Residents of Hershey, Pa should be concerned . . . sales are going down . . .

The once ubiquitous Harvey has disappeared behind the veil again.

I have called two different phone numbers, both disconnected, checked the Internet for ABM Maintenance, called Qwest to have them give me a list of calls to my home phone just to be told 'a court order is required', checked the Internet white pages, no one by his name is listed. All of this and my fate is to be accused of having *abandoned* him again.

My brother's keeper but the keeping is difficult . . .

May 9th & 10th, 2004
Yakima Visit

Cappy is in great spirits because yesterday she saw her two younger sons, Tony and Rick. Gib, Marilyn, Jo and Cappy visited Tony and Rick in Yakima, the mid-sized central Washington city where she spent several decades raising children, working in the fruit warehouses and being a wife to her hard drinking construction worker husband.

Having reestablished her connection with her two boys, Cappy is fully aware Tony and Rick know where she lives now, and has the peace of mind she has been seeking these last few months. Tony and Rick work for the giant Weyerhaeuser Company and their jobs are demanding with a great amount of overtime making it difficult for them to visit their mother half way across the state.

Our visit to Yakima accomplished another immediately important goal. An agreement was reached regarding the issue of the Fairbanks Avenue house. The owners of Cappy's former home are her five surviving children, Gib, Jo, Harvey, Tony and Rick. Four of the five siblings agreed the house should be sold with one dissenting vote.

The dissenting vote belonged to Rick. (Let's be fair. In retrospect, Rick was right!)

A viewing of the house determined that Jason was no longer living there. However, in its present condition the house is uninhabitable. A list was made of all repair work needed to meet minimal requirements for sale of the property. Jo, the family real estate guru, emphasized that an FHA loan would be impossible to qualify for hence, the house would have to be sold under the terms of a private contract.

(Jo, after becoming frustrated because her brothers were dragging their feet regarding the work required to prepare the house for sale, gathered a crew of four and went to Yakima to begin the extensive work needed to be done. She intended to do whatever basic work her crew could accomplish (painting, reseeding the lawn . . . etc . . .) and contract out the rest. Her estimate of cost for all of the work was between $10,000 and $15,000 . . . fortuitously, a neighbor from two houses down, a Hispanic contractor with a growing family, came over and offered to buy the property for $55,000. Roberto purchased the house as it stood, agreed to a $10,000 down payment and the property changed hands. Cappy was elated when she found out the Fairbanks house went to a family with young children. The house is across from Garfield Elementary and a wonderful location for a family. Roberto, the new owner, made incredible improvements to the house and it now stands as the nicest home in the neighborhood.)

May 11th, 2004
Gib provided transport of Fannie to and from Petco for her hair appointment. A couple of hours and fifty dollars and magically, she is transformed. She looks great and seems to have a better attitude due to her improved appearance. However, her girlish figure is a thing of the past . . . age will have its way with all of us.

May 12th, 2004
Cappy is going to get a visit from her third husband, the construction worker, father of Tony, Rick and Jo. He is now retired and living in Arizona with Ruth, his new partner. She is said to be wealthy as a result of accumulated Safeway stock. In years past, his visits have been limited to roughly ten minutes . . . which Cappy with tongue firmly in cheek states is 'about seven minutes too long'.

May 13th, 2004
Jo

Thanks, and you're welcome for the cookie!

Try this one for ABM Janitorial. Hopefully, I found the right one . . . 206-325-1800.

May 14th, 2004
Marilyn, Gib, Jo and Harvey visiting.

Jo

Cappy believes today is Harvey's birthday! After telling her Harvey's birthday isn't until August she suggested we celebrate early. We wished Harvey a Happy Birthday and Cappy sang him two songs popular in her youth, "Poke, Poke, Pokin Along" and "Five Foot Two' intoning melody and lyrics perfectly.

Harvey said she made his day.

Gib

I, as usual in any group large or small, was in the background and no one noticed the moisture in my eyes as I recalled a young Cappy, sixty-one years before, in the kitchen of her small home in North Bonneville, singing to her toddlers, Mickey and Gib . . .

'Mairzy doats and dozy doats and liddle lamzy divey

A kiddley divey too, wooden shoe?'

A little happiness mixed in with black eyes, children being beaten with switches and the Tom Sawyeresque feel of a small town surrounded by the Bonneville Dam, the Columbia River, fishing and swimming holes, and meadows alternately filled with small frogs and wildflowers.

Everything a barefoot boy could want and wonderful people, Tex Eggleston, Peg Erickson, Shorty, the Goodrich boys, Chick, Irene, Butch and Alice, Madsens all . . . wonderful memories but then a monster came to our house at the end of every day, the Cougar, Coug Edmonson. But, those were days fraught with terror, unlike today . . . today was wholly different. We were watching a happy Cappy sing to her children and feeling blessed!

Life Care Center
Cappy now resides at Life Care Center, a nursing home here in Federal Way. She has been at Life Care Center for three months. Her move from Evergreen Lodge became necessary because of continued episodes of dehydration. She 'wasn't thirsty'! We pleaded and cajoled but we could not force fluids on her. But, at Life Care Center she could be more closely monitored and consistent urging to drink water could help stem the bouts of dehydration . . . we hoped.

Last Days
We continue to visit every day. Jo and Marilyn are her mainstays. She never forgets who they are but it becomes different with her son Gib. On good days she knows exactly who he is…at other times he is simply a stranger who stops by to exchange pleasantries with her. He is easily able to discern a good day from a bad day and readily accepts whatever role Cappy ascribes to him. Son or stranger, good spirits and

laughter prevail . . . right up to the day she greets him as 'Gib' and, smiling, declares, 'Gib, I'm going on a trip!'

I smile back and ask, 'Are you flying or walking?'

She replies, 'I don't know yet!'

A pleasant visit followed.

Two and a half hours later her favorite CNA Greg, returned Cappy to her room after dinner. As was usual in these circumstances, Greg and Cappy were trading quips back and forth, whimsical remarks as he helped her into her bed.

One moment a sharing of lighthearted banter and the next she was simply gone, totally unresponsive, as peaceful a transition as anyone could hope for.

No one accurately predicted the emptiness Cappy's passing would create in the coming days and nights of her frequent visitors, Gib, Jo and Marilyn. Had she been difficult for even one day in those last months of her life, each of us might have said . . . *it's time*, but her good spirits, her declaration that 'I just enjoy life' and the ever present smile upon seeing one of us, or all of us, made our incompleteness an absolute, and the assurance that we would one day be whole again, wholly uncertain.

She is with family. Gib senses her nearness and hears her laughter when the simple aspects of life become inordinately more complex . . . and laughs with her. Jo feels the warmth of her mother's support as she diligently applies her property management experience to her new temporary staffing business. She is with Tony and Rick, her Yakima sons in their successful efforts to overcome debilitating illnesses.

The steadfast love and loyalty of Cappy's daughter-in-law Marilyn, over eighteen years, engenders the occasional unbidden smile on her face and she explains 'Mom is visiting' . . . we understand . . .

Short biographies and photographs of the progeny of Roy Zimmer (Cappy's first husband, the miscreant bartender, fruit tramp, pseudo intellectual) are on the following pages.

Part III

BIO's

The people in the short bios below represent success though they are the generational offspring of Roy Zimmer, a man who abandoned his children. The contrasts are apparent. Mike Zimmer, Roy Zimmer's son, often broke the law and ultimately spent time in a federal prison for a violation of the Mann Act. Craig Miller, Mike's son, has been a police officer over many decades in the small city (Yakima, Washington) where both he and his father grew up.

Roy Zimmer's daughter, Victoria Mazelli, never met her father. In a recent year (2015), Victoria was named:

Citizen of the Year for the city of San Diego.

Amanda Emhoff White is an exception; she is not related to Roy Zimmer in any way. Amanda is another example of selfless caring for others. She was a great friend to Cappy and is a great mom to her own children.

Victoria (Zimmer/Unkrey) Mazelli
Born December 2, 1946 to Leroy Albert Zimmer and Verla Mae (Winslow) Zimmer

Verla Mae and Victoria were abandoned by Roy Zimmer prior to Victoria's birth. She never met her father. Verla Mae married Howard Unkrey in November, 1947. Howard Unkrey adopted Victoria and raised her to believe she was his biological daughter. At age eighteen Victoria learned of her mother's previous marriage to Roy Zimmer. Though shaken by this revelation, Victoria's knowledge and love for the man who raised her, never wavered. It was agreed that Roy Zimmer's name would never again be spoken of within the Unkrey family.

A strong will to please her parents led Victoria Into the banking industry. Her 24 years in banking included many responsible positions and she rose from teller to Vice-President of Sales.

In 1985 Victoria met and fell in love with Gary Kent Mazelli. Mazelli owned a highly successful insurance business. Tall, good looking, gentle, Victoria was captivated. She was 38 and Gary was 36. Their son Ryan was born on Valentine's Day in 1987. An idyllic future turned tragic when Gary Mazelli died (January 6th, 1991) in an airplane accident involving his private aircraft. Ryan was not quite 4 years old.

Nothing would be the same for Victoria again.

But, with a strong will, a son to raise and a determination to give Ryan the best opportunities possible, Victoria went back to school and completed a Graphics Arts program. In January of 1996 she started Mazelli Graphics, a successful home-based business. Mazelli Graphics thrived while allowing Victoria to be home with Ryan. Romance was set aside during Ryan's years of school. Mother and son, devoted to each other during this time, became immensely successful.

Next Page: Ryan Mazelli

Ryan Mazelli (Victoria's son/Roy Zimmer's grandson)

Ryan Mazelli worked hard both in and out of school starting at age fourteen. Victoria rewarded her son's hard work with a trip to Europe in 2004. They toured London, Paris and Rome, ending their trip by driving throughout Italy for 11 days, allowing Ryan the opportunity to get a sense of his Italian heritage. Ultimately, in addition to a connection to his 'Italian roots', Ryan was able to meet many family members, his relatives by way of a man he barely knew, his father. Through this travel experience he was imbued with a penchant for travel. In the 14 years since 2004, Ryan has either visited, performed charitable work or had businesses in 36 countries. After the trip to Europe Ryan elected to continue his education at Chapman University just 95 miles down the I-5 corridor from San Diego, in Orange County. He graduated from Chapman in 2009 with a major in Business Finance and a minor in Real Estate.

Victoria describes her son as 'forward thinking, intelligent, highly respected, published in his field, outgoing, generous, fun; an amazing son.' From a distance, a view of Ryan's achievements, supports her conclusions.

Next Page: Amanda (Safeway Angel)

Amanda Emhoff White (Cappy's Safeway Angel)

Cappy's children, all five of them, had children of their own! All five of them had jobs, errands to run, appointments to keep. They were not always available when her cupboards were bare, so she frequently called upon her Safeway Angel to provide some help and a ride. Amanda and Gordie were Cappy's adopted grandchildren. Well, they weren't formerly adopted, but after years of watching over them while Sharon, their mother, worked, Cappy considered them her grandchildren. Once Amanda was grown, she became a meat cutter for Safeway and, not forgetting the care and love Cappy had given her and Gordie, she always made time when Cappy called needing help and a ride to Safeway, the same store where Amanda had just put in a full eight hours. Always there!

When Gib and Marilyn visited Cappy in the Fairbanks house and the cupboards were full, they knew, but Cappy would say, 'Safeway Angel'. Amanda! Young people, fully grown, will often leave a nurturing non-relative behind, forgotten. Not Amanda! Safeway aside, Cappy loved Amanda and Gordie.

Next Page: Jen Saunderson—Comedienne/Roy Zimmer's great granddaughter

Jen Saunderson (Daughter of Lori (Zimmer) Converse
Great granddaughter of Roy Zimmer

Who would guess that this dynamo would emerge from the likes of Roy and Mike Zimmer? However, maybe her mother Lori, her grandmother Rosalie, her great-grandmother Cappy; all had a part in the interaction of genes creating Jen Saunderson, a comedy presence becoming well-known nationally and internationally! Ambitious, irreverent, opinionated and privately a 'bit blue', she is loving the journey.

There is sadness in all families. That her grandfather, the troubled and rebellious Mike Zimmer, Cappy's eldest son, did not live long enough to know his grandchildren, is sad. He would be proud of his daughter Lori, forgiving of his son Michael Dean, and shake his head in amazement and pride . . . at his police officer son, Craig.

And this granddaughter? They would have clashed! They would have fought! Mike would have been a Trump supporter if for no other reason than being against a woman for President. And the *gun* controversy. But, he had a sense of humor, and he and Jen, equally certain and fixed in their beliefs, would have found a middle ground! It would have been explosive! And fun!

Jen and her husband Don are ensconced in Los Angeles, each pursuing a dream. Jen and her uncle, half-brother to her mother Lori, Craig (Miller), are college graduates. A rare achievement among Cappy's clan. Already successful, Jen is reaching for the stars!

Next Page: Michael Dean Zimmer-Son of Michael Zimmer/grandson of Roy Zimmer

Michael Dean Zimmer
(Eldest son of Mike Zimmer)

Ezekiel 18:19-20 "The son shall not suffer for the iniquity of the father."

The iron of his father is missing in Michael Dean. The intent to win all battles, *all battles,* is missing as well. Michael Dean possessed the mien to get through life successfully except for one epic problem, he worshiped his emotionally dysfunctional father. And, too young to sort the wheat from the chaff, he emulated his father's effort to slip fluidly under and around the system, a system that demands that one walk a straight line and do the right thing. He went to prison where he learned a better way. To work, to smile, to not take everything so seriously. And he never returned to any form of incarceration! Life was hard! He'd made the mistake of being tattooed in every skin area visible to the naked eye. His face was covered with tattoo's when he emerged from the *joint*. Meeting Michael Dean for the first time is unsettling because of the tattoos. Ten minutes of conversation with him and his humanity erases the original discomfort of the facial ink. He can laugh at himself and declares that his job is maintaining a beauty salon. He isn't a hairdresser, he keeps the salon clean and running smoothly. On each side of the salon there is a tavern. Does he spend time in the taverns? No, he is afraid that spending time in any tavern will lead to a fight with a bartender, a customer or, laughing as he says it, a barstool! Does he smoke? No! Why not? 'Because I want to keep breathing!' Michael Dean isn't going to head up a corporation but, he is successfully putting one foot in front of the other. Michael Dean is a gifted artist. To date he has not found a way to make that gift contribute to an easier way of life. He lives in a warm climate and finds friends and a compatible relationship now and then. We applaud his will to get through each day with a smile.

Next Page: Craig Miller (Son of Michael Zimmer/Grandson of Roy Zimmer)

Craig Miller
(Mike Zimmer's youngest son/grandson of Roy Zimmer)

The acorn and the tree! This acorn, this achieving son of a miscreant father, lives a life wholly distant from that led by his father. He is an athlete, a college graduate . . . and be easy wherever you're resting Mike Zimmer, he has spent his life working to penalize those of his father's ilk. Craig is a police officer in the midsize city where his father was raised, Yakima, Washington.

In the last three decades of Mike Zimmer's life, he assumed the identity of another person, a man with the common name of Miller. Doing so allowed him to put a wall between himself and the police, and anyone else who might be looking for him with ill intent. The new name also gave him the ability to claim disability and qualify for health insurance, a need that was of extreme necessity as his health continued to decline due to the onset of diabetes and emphysema.

Mike Zimmer's last days were spent in the tenuous security provided by a motorcycle gang. He was cared for by a former prostitute he'd been close to for several decades.

He had little or no contact with his youngest son as his life ebbed away.

And therein lies an issue where Craig Miller is concerned. It seems apparent that Craig, with full justification, resents his father. And apparent also, it seems that Craig's resentment has carried over to anyone named Zimmer.

In his youth, living just a short distance away from Cappy, Craig visited his grandmother often, enjoying a great relationship with her and a casual relationship with her younger sons, Tony and Rick. As time passed, Craig became a star athlete, eventually earning a scholarship to a Utah university as a baseball pitcher with professional potential. Unfortunately, an injury to his pitching arm derailed his path to minor league baseball, and perhaps a major league career.

Those visits to his grandmother ended as his middle-school years began. No one knew why. Craig's reasoning likely was that 'no one cared'. But, his grandmother cared and asked about him often. She was somewhat reclusive. But, everyone knew where she was, the Fairbanks house was known and Cappy was known to live there, and as time went by, Christmas presents, birthday acknowledgements for Craig, accumulated in the home where Cappy lived.

She missed her grandson and asked about him often.

Next Page: Lori Zimmer Converse (Daughter of Michael Zimmer/granddaughter of Roy Zimmer)

Lori Zimmer Converse and daughter Jennifer
(Mike Zimmer's daughter and granddaughter)

Lori! Quiet, almost withdrawn! Up there with the 'greatest moms' ever', Lori Converse needs no flattery, brooks no flattery, is suspicious of a flatterer, she is grounded, hardworking and knows that she is blessed! Her mother Rosalie was kind and loving and Lori misses her mom everyday.

Her daughter, Jen, is an ongoing gift cherished by Lori.

The gifts of Lori's mom and daughter were in sharp contrast to her misgivings of the infrequent presence of her father, Michael Roy Zimmer. Lori's father, from his earliest days, had difficulty with the tumult of his existence. Abandoned by his own biological father, beaten by his first stepfather and under the constant threat of violence from his second stepfather, Mike Zimmer didn't know who to trust. Apparently, no one!

He simply repeated the errors of his own father. He pretty much ignored his children. Lori's uncle simplified the formula when he said, "Zimmer women are near perfect, Zimmer men are flawed! For confirmation of that conclusion, Gib says, 'Look at the evidence! Kari, his daughter, virtually perfect, Victoria (Roy's daughter, Gib and Mike's sister) virtually perfect, Lori, virtually perfect, Jen traveling in Japan as this is written doing comedy, entertaining, virtually perfect!

The father, Roy Zimmer . . . epically flawed! His progeny Mike and Gib, admittedly flawed. Michael Dean, Mike's son, been to prison, the tattooed man, apparent flaws, Mark Zimmer, Gib's son, charming, articulate, knowledgeable but, like his father, the armor is chipped, the halo markedly askew, he smokes and has been known to have a drink or two. Analysis, like most Zimmer men, definitively flawed!

Two exceptions! Craig Miller and Ryan Mazelli. Maybe they have flaws unknown to us? Maybe . . .

Next Page: Mark Zimmer, Cappy and Kari Pitharoulis(Daughter and son of Gary

(Gib) Zimmer (grandson and grandaughte of Roy Zimmer)

Mark Zimmer, Cappy, Kari Pitharoulis
(Gib's daughter and son/Cappy's grandchildren)

Kari

Just another pretty face? No! Kari thinks, adopts worthy causes *and becomes active.* Employee of the Year for the City of Olympia, Washington, paralegal extraordinaire, business-owner (with husband Jeff), master of light humor and always, always there for those of us prone to indiscretion!

Cappy and Charlene (Gib's first wife) shared a bond not wholly unique to mother-in-laws and daughter-in-laws, *but rare*. The closeness, the understanding between them, was easily seen by all. Then Charlene gave birth to Kari. Kari's entry into the world was a true blessing to Cappy! As Kari grew and became the articulate teen and then young adult, when the three of them were in the same room, others knew that love and humor unusual to three women, was present.

Magic! When Charlene and Gib's marriage faltered (due to the well-known and acknowledged flaws common to most male Zimmer's) the close bond between Cappy and Charlene remained, enriched and heightened by Kari.

Mark

Mark is a collector! He collects information like the south collects birds in winter. He stores it and relates it back to anyone he believes worthy of sharing with him. He collects friends and he doesn't let them go. A telephone within reach is his instrument for sharing books, movies and concerts. If it's of interest to him then it must be of interest to everyone. If not, it should be! He embraces physically, emotionally, intellectually.

He can sense hostility and he smiles and quietly walks away.

He is a video game guy! His mastery of games goes way back, Defender, Galaga, Asteroids and graduating to Doom, Resident Evil and Borders. The more complex the better.

Managed a Game Stop store for years.

Loves his mom! Envelops her, protects her every way imaginable to man.

He is a male Zimmer. A few beers and the rawness of his flaws begin to appear. He is right and knows absolutely that he can convince you to *see the light*.

The flaws are there. He is his father's son and is besotted with the gift of life; and he knows his mission is to explore all aspects of that gift. And will patiently *share* what he has learned, with those who have yet to learn.

He does so, *most* often, with a light touch, until the teaching, hence the learning, fails to enlighten, then he will smile and turn away from anyone unwilling to receive his gift.

Unless, that someone is his sister. She believes, and it is so true, that he can *learn from her,* if only he would pause, open his mind. Her jaw is set! He smiles and another torrent of words flow forth, and she relents! There is no hope! He is insufferable! She loves him ... tomorrow is another day! Maybe the wisdom of a woman whose last name many years ago was *Zimmer,* with all that that implies, will penetrate this blessed brother of hers. Maybe not!

He is Cappy's grandson and he mirrors many of her traits! Laughs easily, is discerning, understanding, caring. Mark is cherished by his family as Cappy was by her family. One needs only see the picture above of Kari, Mark and Cappy . . . a sharing of love that still exists.

Cappy is still with her children and her grandchildren.

End

www.ingramcontent.com/pod-product-compliance
Lightning Source LLC
Chambersburg PA
CBHW061222070526
44584CB00029B/3946